L E R A

L E R A

by
Lerthansung
with
Stanley Scism

Lera

by Lerthansung with Stanley Scism

©1987 Word Aflame Press
Hazelwood, MO 63042-2299

Cover Design by Tim Angew

All Scripture quotations in this book are from the King James Version of the Bible unless otherwise identified.

All rights reserved. No portion of this publication may be reproduced, stored in an electronic system or transmitted in any form or by any means, electronic, mechanical, photocopy, recording, or otherwise, without the prior permission of Word Aflame Press. Brief quotations may be used in literary reviews.

Printed in United States of America.

Printed by

Library of Congress Cataloging-in-Publication Data

Lerthansung, 1927-
   Lera: the miraculous ministry of a national missionary in northeast India / by Lerthansung, as told to Stanley Scism.
     p.   cm.
   ISBN 0-932581-24-2 :
   1. Lerthansung, 1927- . 2. Missionaries—India. Northeastern—
Biography.   I. Scism,Stanley, 1958- . II. Title.
BV3269.L43A3 1987
266'.994'0924—dc 19
[B]   87-23171
                                                                           CIP

Contents

	Foreword 7
	Preface 11
1.	Boyhood 13
2.	Coming to God 25
3.	Spiritual Power 41
4.	Spiritual Preparation 49
5.	Senvon, Manipur 57
6.	Churachandpur, Manipur 67
7.	East Manipur 77
8.	Cachar 89
9.	Divine Protection 95
10.	Cachar II 101
11.	Tripura 107
12.	North Cachar Hills 113
13.	Shillong, Meghalaya 115
14.	Establishing the Missions Department 119
15.	Mikir Hills 123
16.	Nagaland 127
17.	Andaman Islands 143
18.	Bangladesh 145
19.	Sikkim 161
20.	West Bengal 165
21.	Bhutan 173
22.	Nepal 179
23.	Arunachal Pradesh 183
24.	Calcutta 191
25.	Garo Hills 197
26.	South Tripura 203
27.	The Philippines, Japan, and Thailand 207

28. Mainland India I 217
29. Mainland India II.........................231
30. Missions Work in 1986 251
31. My Family Through the Years 259
32. Spiritual Children and Spiritual Volleyball ...269

Maps

Northeast India 24
Mizoram 40
India 216

Foreword

The hill people of Northeast India migrated to India from other areas of Southeast Asia. Some believe that these interesting tribal people now generally known as Mizos originally came from southern China, eventually moving into Burma and finally India. They are indeed unique, both from the standpoint of their culture and from the standpoint of their historical background. As people who have struggled for survival, facing many severe hardships, they have developed a tremendous strength of character, determination, and community spirit.

It has been my privilege to be associated closely with these people for about thirty-five years. As a young missionary, the contribution I was able to make in helping them was more than compensated for by the tremendous lessons they taught me. My respect and appreciation for them is very great. These tribal people taught me how to submit to God and in simple faith believe God for the miraculous. Their childlike faith has produced the reward of an unusual demonstration of the Holy Spirit in their lives and ministry. The contents of this book are no surprise, for I have personally witnessed unusual manifestations of God at work among these believing people.

Standing tall among these Spirit-filled, Bible-loving tribal people is a man short in stature by the name of Pastor Lerthansung. He is commonly known as Lera and has pioneered new districts in Northeast India. He is now busily engaged as the general missions director in opening new fields of missionary work. The Northeast Indian church stands behind him with strong sacrificial giving,

Foreword

making this unusual missionary program possible. How moving it is to see these people who have so little of this world's goods give of their poverty in order to evangelize the world.

From a very early age our son, Stanley, has associated with these people. As a minister he has been privileged to travel and preach with Pastor Lerthansung. How thrilled we are that he has now, as a co-author, had a part in preparing the story of one of these spiritual giants living in a remote area of the world.

It is my prayer that this story of God's work among people of childlike faith will enhance the reader's faith and will encourage each one to reach out for the miraculous in his or her own life, for indeed, God is no respecter of persons.

    Harry E. Scism
    Director of Foreign Missions
    United Pentecostal Church International

* * * * * * * * *

It was my privilege to meet Brother Lerthansung in the middle or late 1950s in the town of Aizawl, where I had journeyed from South India to attend the annual United Pentecostal Church conference of what was then known as the Lushai Hills. He had arrived from the Manipur area, having graduated from a Bible school located there, and was selling medical supplies to help support himself while preaching. He knew some English, which enabled us to become better acquainted. He ultimately affiliated with the UPC and is one of our many

Foreword

fine, faithful, loyal preachers in India today.

After his affiliation I requested him to assume the responsibility of district pastor of Manipur District, and this he did. Later it was my privilege to fly to Imphal and be met there by Brother Lerthansung and others. A church had been established in New Churachandpur, and I went to attend the district conference. We did what we could to provide some personal support as well as funds for the district. He was given a bicycle and a typewriter, which became a great asset since his alphabet is the same as that used in English.

Brother Lerthansung eventually moved with his family to Fullertol, near Lakhipur on the plains of Assam. I attended several conferences in this new district, making a special trip there to purchase property for his home and church. He has been consistent in his walk with God and in the fellowship of his brethren through the years and has opened additional areas to the good news.

I have many fond memories of services together as well as of amusing incidents. I have found this fine brother to be humble, not self-assertive, and willing to serve in any capacity.

E. L. Scism
Former Superintendent
United Pentecostal Church of India

* * * * * * * *

The year 1955 was memorable to me, as it was the first time that I met that brave soldier for the kingdom of God, Brother Lerthansung. Since then, I have admired

Foreword

and appreciated very, very much his devotedness to God and to the preaching of God's Word. From 1960 to the present we have labored together for God and carried many responsibilities in the service of the church of God. I was very delighted when I saw his great determination and keen interest to win souls to the Word of God. It is a great privilege for the United Pentecostal Church of Northeast India to have such a minister as Brother Lerthansung, who is a stalwart soldier of the cross and a true servant of God. We are very thankful for him.

Brother Lerthansung is one of the early, great pioneers who carried the revival of Pentecost to parts of Northeast India, Bangladesh, Bhutan, and the Andaman Islands. In his ministry to date he has baptized 5,500 souls in the name of Jesus, and he has founded three districts, eight mission fields, and more than fifty churches. Moreover, God has given him a great talent in the art of teaching, and this has produced good results and great fruit in the ministry of our Bible school students in different spheres. He presently serves as general missions director of Northeast India.

I am very grateful to Sister Allan Shalm and Brother Stanley K. Scism who began and have completed a great work in publishing the life history of Brother Lerthansung.

Finally, I hope that everyone who reads this book will receive a great blessing and new life from the great adventures of this brave soldier of God.

K. Satinvela
General Superintendent
United Pentecostal Church of Northeast India

Preface

This book had two beginnings. In 1984 Allan Shalm asked Brother Lerthansung, whose nickname is Lera, to write his life's story. This work he began, with his daughters helping him on the typing and Georgene Shalm helping with English grammar. In 1985, not knowing that wheels had already been set in motion, I asked Lerthansung to dictate on cassette his life's story, adding that I would transcribe the tapes, straighten up the grammar without tampering with his style, and try to get the manuscript printed. In April 1986, on the Andaman Islands, I had the chance to interview him for this book. After recording six cassettes, Lerthansung patiently listened to the first five, writing down spellings for names of people and places he had mentioned.

As I transcribed the tapes, I realized that certain explanations would be necessary but wanted to make these without intrusion on Lera's style. Thus brackets and parentheses have been used to separate my comments from his and keep both styles pure. All comments in brackets and parentheses are mine, coming either from personal recollection or from interviews with E. L. Scism, Harry Scism, Audrene Scism, Lerthansung, Satinvela, or Chunga.

Some of Lerthansung's story comes from his original brief written account, and a very little is from an update he sent me in January 1987, but the majority comes from the tapes. Where the written and taped accounts conflicted, I usually took the written account regarding facts and figures, which would be more difficult to remember

Preface

on the spur of the moment during a recording. When emotional matters such as personal conversations and relationships are involved, I have relied on the cassettes to demonstate the natural human sense of drama. I have also borne in mind that in India written English tends to be more stilted than standard English usage worldwide.

Brother Lerthansung and I are both very grateful to Brother Allan Shalm's beginning this project by his initial suggestion and encouragement and for the tireless work of Sister Allan (to use the Northeast Indian manner of speech) on the first written manuscript. Thanks also are due to Sister Mary Wallace and Sister Thetus Tenney, who encouraged my work on this project. I thank my parents, Brother Harry Scism and Sister Audrene Scism, for giving me, by their continual involvement, spiritual wisdom and Christian character, the chance not only to be born and brought up in India as a missionary kid but also to observe as a child and as a young man the example of what a missionary ought to be.

The final and greatest gratitude goes to Jesus Christ, who has made all these lives and this work possible.

Stanley Scism

1 (1927-1941)
Boyhood

My name is Lerthansung Tryte, but in my childhood we never used our surnames. For this reason even now when I write a letter I sign it simply Lerthansung.

I was born in January 1927 in Senvon Village, Manipur State, India, near the Burma border. (Manipur is in Northeast India. This entire region was formerly known as Assam; now Assam is the name of the largest of several states there.)

The village of Senvon is perched on top of a hill for several reasons, chiefly for the good defensive position it commanded in the days of tribal war. During the time of tribal war, which was before the British came, every village, large or small, was surrounded by a line of large beams of timber. The village gates were opened during the day and closed at sundown. After Christianity came and the tribal wars were suppressed, the country became free from attack and the blockades were removed.

I belong to the Hmar tribe, which is one of many tribes known generally as Mizo, meaning hill people. (The term

Lera

Mizo is now also used in a narrower sense to mean the people and language formerly called Lushai, who inhabit Mizoram State.) In general the Hmar people have cultural and physical resemblances to the rest of the mountain people of Northeast India and Burma. We are generally a short and sturdy race of men with good development of muscle; our face is broad and round, and our cheekbones are high, broad, and prominent. Our eyes are small and our nose flat and short. Though we are of the Mongoloid race, our skin is not yellow but rather a yellowish brown.

When I was born, our village contained about 350 houses. At that time our houses were very simple. For roofs we used sun grass. For floors we used bamboo. For posts we used trees. Generally there were no partitions inside the house. Usually there were two doors—one in the front and another in the back. There were few windows. The house was a little high—from the earth about four feet. Sometimes we could fall through the floor to the earth if the floor wasn't so good. Under the house, whatever animals we had—buffaloes, cattle, chickens, dogs, pigs—all lived together. We had no bathroom. At night we never went outside to pass water; we simply made a hole in the floor. My father always said, "No need to go outside."

[E.L. Scism, when he traveled into the Northeast Indian hills in spreading the Oneness truth and founding the United Pentecostal Church, stayed in many similar homes. In recalling his visits to Senvon and Rawkot, a village three to four miles away, he mentions that the smoke from the kitchen area would permeate the entire home until it yellowed the mosquito net, an item necessary to prevent malaria. He would sit by the window in homes like Lerthansung's, eyes watering, "hoping for fresh air to enter the premises and allay discomfort." He also points out that the presence of functioning animals directly beneath gave "room for odors to rise to the living area."]

We had no factory-made cotton cloth in those days. All our young people made cotton cloth; we worked it ourselves. (Throughout Manipur, cotton cording and spinning was customary and a cottage industry.)

Almost the entire population of our people can still be classified as agriculturists or cultivators. Generally our people shift their jhum (field) every year. Every year a farmer cultivates another jhum. First, he selects a tract of land and fells all the bamboo and trees on the tract. When the bamboo and trees are completely dried, he sets fire to the land. Then he sows grain and vegetables. The jhum is good only for one year; the next year the farmer must start all over again in another region. The main crop is rice. (Manipur grows the best rice in India, which is saying a lot.)

Our people's food is cooked rice. We eat three heavy meals a day of almost identical preparation; all other meals are of little significance. The men generally will eat almost any kind of meat—domestic animals or wild creatures such as monkeys and rats—but the women are much more discriminating.

[Ellis Scism explains that usually the undergrowth in fields was cut off, while the mammoth trees remained. There was no plowing; the hillsides were too steep for large machinery. Farmers would dig holes and plant three to five seeds in each one. After one season of cultivation, the land would lie fallow and the jungle would take over until a few years later, when cultivation would return to the same plot again. As for the food produced and prepared, northeastern curries are usually quite mild in comparison to the spicy and often fiery food of the plains. The cultivation and preparation of this food affected a child's daily life.]

Our fathers and mothers were very busy in farm work. In the evening when our mothers came from the jhum, they would supply us milk. We had no other milk and no sugar. In the daytime, generally we simply had water. Sometimes our elder sisters would chew food in their mouths and supply us from their mouths. We had buffaloes and cows, but at that time we never thought of their milk as good for us. Our only object in raising them was to kill them. (Saving the milk for calves increased the herd, and since this area wasn't Hindu, slaughtering cattle violated no religious scruples.)

We were very dirty. We never washed. Sometimes adults took baths two or three times in a month. However, we children had no clothes, and our mothers and fathers said, "If we have them take a bath every day, surely they will die." So we never took baths. In the mountains, the weather never approached the heat of the plains, and it could get quite cold indoors or out. Also, the people had to pack water in hollowed out bamboo receptacles, or in four-gallon kerosene tins, a long way up the ridge to the village. Generally, when the rain came, we children would simply run out in the street. This was our bath. We never went to the river or water hole, so the rains were very convenient.

During my childhood, we were very, very free. At mealtime, our parents would say what they wanted to say, but that was all. Then they went to the jungle or to the field, and the whole day we were free. Wherever we wanted, we could go and play with our friends. I was usually interested in playing under the thick forest. We made traps for birds. We combined leaves into shoes that we could use for one day—a one-day shoe.

[E. L. Scism points out that among Indian children social life had "no hindrances" since a lack of competition in the Western sense allowed them to be "happy irrespective of what they had, and they had few playthings which our American society must give to youngsters to keep them contented."]

In the nighttime, we all gathered together. Sometimes we ate together. We would tell our friends, "Please bring your food and curry. I also will bring my food and curry." While gathering together we often joked or played or fought.

[Audrené Scism says, "Curry is a hot, spicy dish which can be made of meat, chicken, fish, or vegetables. It is usually used as a gravy that is ladled over the rice. Chutneys and lime or mango pickles often accompany the meal."]

From 1927 to 1933, whenever the family went into the village, my mother carried me on her back.

[That custom continues. A cloth is thrown around the child and over one shoulder of the mother. E. L. Scism says that these hasty arrangements render the baby at times "not well covered as far as the rear section is concerned." To accommodate mothers who carried babies on their backs, our church benches have no backs. A fussy child can be quieted by the mother gently rocking backward and forward to appease the "situations internal and external."]

When the Mizo people have a drink, they do not want to drink by themselves. In the nighttime they gather together to drink. When I was a child, my mother brought me to the place where the people drank. There I had my first "sweet" drink at about seven years of age.

[Smoking also begins at a young age in Northeast India. Young people roll their own cigarettes, and women sometimes smoke pipes equipped with a water bowl. After the nicotine drops down into the water, they give it to their husbands to drink.]

Our people have only a few musical instruments. Gongs and drums are the most popular ones. We have flutes made of bamboo, and another very popular instrument is the leaf of a tree. Any young man can play nicely from a tree leaf.

We hill people like very much to sing, and we have composed many songs. After we became Christians, many people composed songs to worship the Lord. Also, after being baptized with the Holy Ghost, we received spiritual songs from on high, and now we can sing nicely under the control of the Holy Spirit. We hill people are very fond of dancing, and we have many kinds of dances. Since we became Christians, we now worship the Lord with dancing.

[Among the UPC hill people, often an entire local congregation will sing in tongues together. This they call "spiritual songs" and consider it as obedience to Ephesians 5:19. Individual styles of dancing vary considerably, but in church the hill people usually dance in a circle, for which a large vacant space is provided between the pulpit and the first row of benches.]

Up to age twelve, I was never separated from my mother at nighttime. I slept with my parents. In the nighttime we requested our mothers to tell us ghost stories or folk tales.

In about 1910, the first four or five people in the village became Christians after some evangelists came from Mizoram. There were very few Christians of any kind anywhere in those days. In every house people worshiped demons. When we had stomach pains, we called a heathen priest—a man devoted to an evil spirit. We killed animals—chickens, dogs, and other things also— to please the demons. My parents sacrificed many times for my stomach pain, and dedicated me to the demons along with the animals. During that time we had no medicine. And we did not yet know how to pray.

Although my parents were not Christians, I had a desire to be a Christian. In 1933, a mission school started in our village: My father, who was illiterate requested that I be allowed to go to the mission school. I enrolled in the mission school to learn the alphabet.

Every morning we had devotions in our school. The teachers were Indians. We called them evangelistic teachers because they worked as both evangelists and teachers. They worked very hard for the Lord. Our teacher taught us how to pray. He said, "Every morning when you go to take food [eat] you must pray like this: 'Lord, we give thanks. You gave us food, and we thank You.' When you go to bed, say, 'Lord, tonight I am going to bed. Please help me sleep.' Like this you must pray simple prayers to Jesus."

Sometimes we memorized Bible verses. Our teacher taught us the story of Jesus as well as Old Testament

Lera

stories. We also learned how to sing. We didn't know Christian songs; we had only heard heathen songs. From our school we learned Christian songs and we learned how to pray.

The teachers forced all the students to enroll in the mission Sunday school. Our teacher said, "You must go to Sunday school on Sunday. This is compulsory for all students. If you do not enroll in the Sunday school, you cannot be admitted into the day school." Thus they took advantage of us.

When I enrolled in the Sunday school, the master wrote down my name and added me to the department list. "Now that we have written your name down, you are a Christian," he said. From that time, I thought, Oh, I am a Christian. In Sunday school we learned more Bible verses and Old Testament stories. Our Sunday school teacher taught us that there is a heaven and a great lake of fire, that all Christians would go to heaven, and that all unbelievers would go to the lake of fire.

All the children wanted to enroll in the school, and to do so they became "Christians." I asked the authorities to register my name as a Christian. After that, I no longer wanted those evil offerings and sacrifices when I got sick. Instead, I prayed to God as best as I could. The students tried to convince their brothers and sisters to become Christians. Some years later, the fathers and mothers became Christians.

We carried our books to school, but we had no slates or exercise books. We made our first slates from planks and used charcoal to write on them. Our teachers taught us to write the ABCs and to read. School lasted from 10:00 AM to 3:00 PM.

Boyhood

Sometimes we had physical exercises. We liked this very much: right turns, left turns, marching. This was a new experience for us. Sometimes we had chorus. We learned many, many choruses in English.

After we became students it was compulsory to go to the river every Saturday to take baths and to wash our clothes. At that time we each had only one pair of pants, so we had to wash our pants, hang them in the sunshine and then lie in the jungle until they dried.

We would play in the jungle, lie around in the jungle, and pray in the jungle. About two hundred yards from the village we were free. But in the nighttime, tigers and other animals sometimes came into the village and attacked the dogs and pigs. When a tiger came, all the people would wake up and go together into the jungle with torches. The fire would frighten the tiger, and we make a great noise shouting, shouting, shouting. We could tell that a tiger was nearby or was coming by the crying of the other animals; they made a great sound. In some places we knew by the smell, for the tiger has a strong smell. At that time there were not only tigers but also small jungle jackals.

There are many pythons in this area. Generally they live under the thick forest and in the valley near the river bank. Pythons are not like other snakes; many of them are not aggressive and it is easy to kill them with an axe. Then we can eat their meat. Our forefathers said that if we eat python meat, we will never suffer cholera. "Very good protection," they said. For that reason we like pythons very much.

But some pythons are very, very dangerous. When a python catches an animal, it tries to put its tail in the

Lera

rectum of the animal. Then it can kill the animal easily.

In one village in 1965 one of our UPC members named Neithang went to the jungle to cut bamboo. When he went down to the river, a big python attacked him. The python bit his leg. He was able to pry its mouth open, but he was still in danger of being killed by the python's tail. He cried loudly for help. At last, he caught hold of the python's tail and bent it in two places. Then the python no longer had power to kill him, but Brother Neithang could not move. Soon some brothers came to help him and killed the python. However, half of Brother Neithang had already died; he was crushed and paralyzed from the waist down.

The sectional presbyter, Brother Pauneilien, and I went to pray for him. Many people were thinking, Brother Neithang will surely die. But when we anointed him in the name of Jesus, Brother Neithang was completely healed.

In 1938 I passed lower class three, ranking sixth in the class. I started upper classes in 1939, and by the help of God, in 1941 I passed middle English class six. This was the highest class in our village; there was no high school. Unfortunately, during this year my mother was suffering from sickness. We spent all our money for sacrifices to the priest and therefore had no money for my school books. Every day after school I carried firewood from the jungle and sold it to earn money for books. Even then I could purchase only one mathematics exercise book. For my other subjects I copied by hand from the books of my friend. But by the grace of our Lord Jesus, I passed middle class six in 1941 at the top of the class.

During this time, we started Boy Scouts in our village.

Boyhood

I worked as a troop leader. Every night we had scout drilling and learned to signal in Morse code. If we had an urgent need to inform another village, we often sent Morse signals by flashlight at nighttime. We could not send a letter, so this was very convenient.

If a person from our village wanted to go to high school, he had to go to another area. The Indo-Burma Bible Mission gave me a monthly stipend of thirteen rupees to go. (Rupees, abbreviated Rs, are the units of Indian currency. At present, the exchange rate fluctuates around thirteen rupees to the U.S. dollar). But when I started high school, the Second World War came and our teacher said, "War is coming. We cannot continue our school. All students must go back to their homes." So I went back to my home, unable to continue my high school studies due to the Second World War.

A little Manipuri boy like Lerthansung once was.

Lera

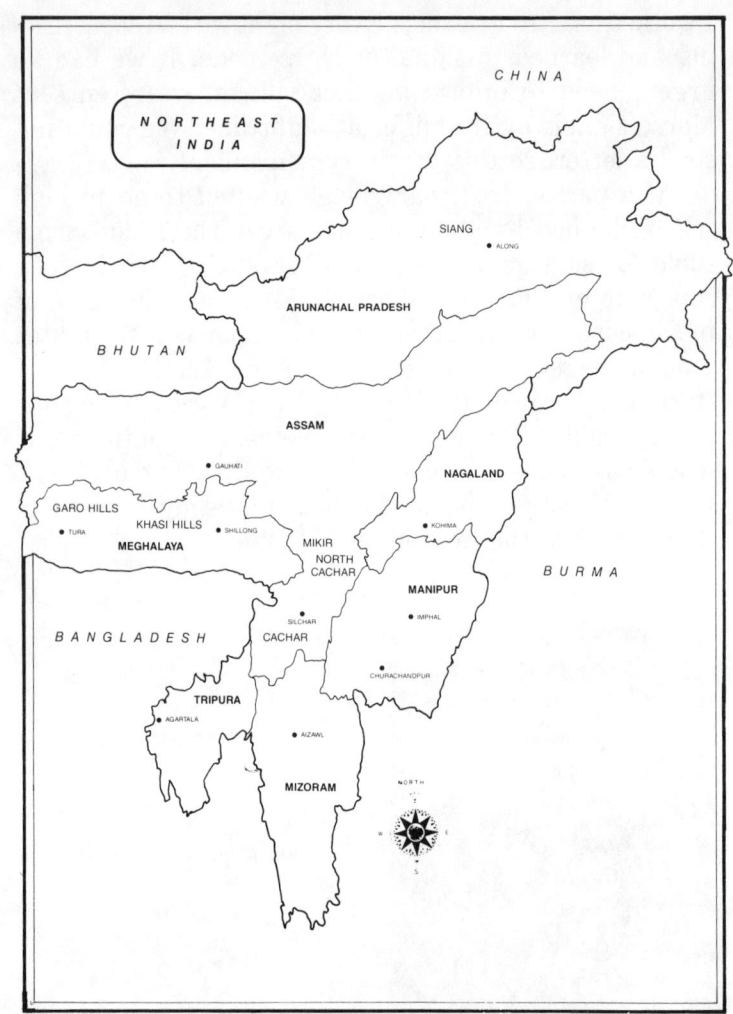

Northeast India

2 (1941-1953)

Coming to God

From 1941 to 1942 I helped my family as a cultivator in the jhum. I also worked as a teacher in Sunday school, where we learned choir and tonic sol-fa. The Sunday School Union conducted open-air meetings on Sunday night, and we tried to convert our parents to Christianity. During this time our parents were still unbelievers: they worshiped idols and demons, and every night they gathered together to drink alcohol and sing worldly songs. When we told them about heaven and the lake of fire, they didn't want to pay attention and would not believe that there was a heaven and a lake of fire. Not only that, when we told them about airplanes, they refused to believe that machines could fly in the air like birds. "Your book is completely wrong," they insisted. Many old men did not believe there were other villages beyond our village.

In 1943 I wanted to go somewhere to learn English. Since I had not been able to continue my high school education, I could not speak English well, but I needed to speak English well because I wanted to become an interpreter. At that time, the British army came to our place, but we could not speak to them. All the people said, "You already passed class six. You must speak to them." As much as I could, I did.

My desire to learn to speak English was so great that I thought, If I can join the Assam Regiment, I might have a better chance to learn English. I went to the Syhlet recruiting office (Syhlet is now in Bangladesh), but the officials there told me, "You must wait. After one week our officer will come. Then he will interview you."

After one week the recruiting officer came and I told him. "Officer, I want to go into the army."

He made measurements. "Ah, you are very young." (I was sixteen). "Also, at this time we need men who are at least five feet two inches. Around the waist we need at least twenty-six inches." In height they accepted me, but my waist was only about twenty-one inches. Then the recruiting officer said, "Boy, we cannot accept you this time. Next year you may come again. I will give you an unfit warrant, which will let you travel for free in trains and buses back to your village."

On my return journey I stopped at a rest camp. There were American soldiers, British soldiers, and Indian soldiers—many soldiers were roaming here and there. I went to the reception desk for the soldiers, and a lady there asked, "Why did you come to this place? You are a civilian. This is a military camp. Get out! Get out!"

I showed my unfit warrant. "Oh, sister, I also want to join the army. I had an interview with an officer, but he said I was unfit. Here is my unfit warrant."

When she saw it, she was so happy. "Oh, so you tried to become a soldier, but since you were unfit you had to return. You are qualified to take a cup of tea, some bread, and anything else you need to eat." She gave me bananas, food, and other things. Since I had an unfit warrant, I enjoyed my journey. After that, I returned to the city of Silchar, Cachar District, Assam State.

When I reached Silchar, I tried to join what we called the civilian army, but there was no vacancy. After two days, I reached the town of Lakhipur.

There I heard news that many sweeper jobs were open at Kumbirgram Airfield, which was about sixteen miles from Silchar. Instead of returning home, I went along with my friends to the airfield to interview for the sweeper job.

It was not difficult to get a job as sweeper. My friends and I were hired and were sent to Camp Two. There were about eighty-five sweepers in Camp Two. I was appointed as leader among the sweepers because I could speak a little English and Hindi. Our salary was Rs 1.50 per day. The next day we were all busy making our own brooms out of bamboo. Our main work was to look after the camp and clean the latrines. We were very busy morning and evening, but we were so happy to have jobs as sweepers.

One day we heard an alarm ring repeatedly. All the soldiers and sweepers were in danger, and each one tried to save his own life by hiding in a trench. My friends and I ran as fast as we could, sometimes rolling, falling and tumbling upside down. Finally we found an empty trench. We quickly jumped in and closed our ears with our fingers. Shortly afterward, we heard a great sound from on high, and saw more than eighty Japanese bombers in the air. They started bombing the airfield, causing a great noise. We couldn't sit properly, and we sometimes fell flat on the ground. We lost all hope of surviving. At last I cried out, "Lord Jesus, save me! Save me!"

After one hour, the bombers left. When we came out of the trench, we saw many ambulances on the airfield carrying dead bodies. I had never seen so many dead bodies in my life. Many people had died, but fortunately our group was OK. A friend said, "If we stay here in Kumbirgram, the Japanese will come again. It is not so good. Very hopeless. We must go away from this airfield." We wanted to leave the airfield as soon as possible. Fortunately, there was no more work for us sweepers, so we left. I did not want to dream of such a terrible thing again. I left with my friends. We reached Lakhipur, and then I turned toward my village.

From Lakhipur to Senvon is not an easy trip. There is no passable road, not even for a jeep. There is a river, so it is possible to go by small boat, but the journey takes about five or six days. The distance is about 150 miles.

We started to walk through the thick forest. In some places we saw jungle elephants and tigers. After eight days we reached safely our village of Senvon. There I heard that many laborers were needed as porters to work on constructing a road between Silchar and Aizawl. (Aizawl is the capital of Mizoram State, an area formerly known as the Lushai Hills.) At that time, no vehicles ran between Silchar and Aizawl, so people had to carry their loads on their heads.

I went to Vairengte Village in Mizoram with some friends to enroll in the labor corps. The monthly wage was Rs 71.50 (about $5.50). Every day we carried about twenty-five kilograms between Vairengte and Bilkhawthlir villages. These loads were sometimes rice, sometimes other things. After two months, since there was no more work to do, I went back to my village with the little money I had earned.

While I was in Mizoram, a doctor who had come from England visited our camp every week. Some people told him, "Lerthansung was in class six, so he can speak English. He needs to speak to our doctor." I was thinking, If I passed middle class six, why can't I speak to English people? Then I thought, Because I did not go to high school.

When I spoke with the doctor, he said, "You are a young boy, and you can speak good English. If you want to come to England, I will take you with me. There you can study further and go to high school."

When he told me this, I was so happy. My uncle came to the labor corps, and I asked him, "Uncle, what to do? This doctor wants to take me to England for further study. If I can, it is good to visit another country."

My uncle answered, "If we do not get advice from or talk to your father and brother and sister, that is not so good. When we go back to our village, then talk to your father and brother and sister. If they agree, you will go to England." But when I went back to our home town, my family did not allow me to go anywhere. So I lost my opportunity.

When I reached my village, I heard that all the Japanese had left Burma. This was in 1943. I invited my friend, Lalthanlien, to visit Tiddim, Burma, to sell some things. In Silchar, I purchased some cloth and some other goods. Both of us carried big baskets full of a variety of goods and set out for Tiddim, which was more than two hundred miles from our village. After spending sixteen days by foot on the way, we reached our destination. I later noted in my diary, "I think that the reason for my small figure is the heavy loads I used to carry on my head during my teens."

What we had in our baskets was the right thing for the people of Tiddim. In no time we sold out. In Silchar I had spent only forty-five rupees to purchase the goods, but I got more than three hundred in sales. So much profit!

It is twelve miles from Tiddim, Burma, to Thantrang. During the war, thousands and thousands in the Japanese army had died in that area. Some people had told me, "The Japanese like very much to make false teeth. Some young men have false teeth made of gold, some of silver, at great expense."

We thought, If we can get two or three false teeth made of gold, we will be very successful. Then three friends and I went beyond Tiddim Village, on a hill where there had been a great battle. When we reached the site, the decaying bodies of the Japanese army were on the ground. When we saw them, we were so happy, saying, "Today we must try to find false teeth made of gold." We got a strong stick, opened their mouths, and held the stick inside their mouths while we checked them one by one. I myself checked more than one hundred soldiers' mouths. The smell was very bad.

Unfortunately, we did not find any false teeth made of gold, so we finally decided to leave. Since the Japanese army had many rifles and bullets, we took some and shot birds and other things also on the way back. We were so happy.

At that time, tigers were hunting in the area. They

were so happy. Not only tigers, but jackals and other predators also came together to eat the flesh of the thousands of dead Japanese soldiers.

This was the last battle in Burma. After that, the Japanese went back to their own country. The Japanese had simple uniforms, much more simple than our expectations. We hadn't even been able to get any false teeth from the Japanese army. So we went back to Tiddim.

From Tiddim we returned to India. We traveled through Mizoram, and after spending some nights there, we came back to our home town. We returned to our village by a shortcut. The roads were infested with wild animals and many leeches sucked us.

[Leeches crawl on leaves of jungle plants during the monsoon season. When a person rushes by and brushes against the foliage, they cling to his clothing. Then they crawl to a place where they can bury their heads in his skin and begin to suck his blood. If he simply pulls them off, they break and their heads remain imbedded in his flesh so that the wounds bleed profusely. Experienced travelers carry salt wrapped up in a bit of newspaper; periodically they stop and sprinkle a pinch of salt on the leeches. Since leeches, like many slugs, can't tolerate salt, they writhe away and remove their heads from the skin. The sufferer can then flick them off his body.]

Sleeping under the thick forest on the way, we arrived safely at our village. I reported to our people about our unsuccessful attempt to find gold teeth in the dead Japanese army. "If we could have gotten two or three made of gold, it would have been profitable, but unfortunately we could not find any." All the people laughed and laughed.

Lera

I now had some money, so I planned to go to high school. My elder brother was getting married, however, and according to our custom all my money was needed for the price of my elder brother's wife. We spent all my money, so I could not continue my business or enroll in high school.

Since my plans to learn English had not been successful, I decided to become an evangelistic teacher. I went to Pherzawl Village in October 1944 and submitted my humble application to the secretary of the standing committee. That time, God arranged it. Since I had passed English in first place in our area, the Presbyterian Independent Church of India appointed me as an evangelistic teacher in Hmongzungkai Village, to start work in January 1945. My pay was five rupees (almost forty cents) per month, but I was happy. I had nothing to complain about; I was content.

The school was twelve miles from my village; I could reach it in one day. I traveled through the thick forest. At that time there were many tigers, and it was very dangerous to go there without a weapon. Sometimes we took a spear, and those who had guns took guns. Since I had no gun, I took a spear. If a tiger came, if necessary I was ready to fight. In addition to tigers, the jungle also contained many snakes and leeches.

I worked as a schoolteacher until 1947. During this period, I taught the younger ones to sing gospel songs. Also, I organized Boy Scouts classes, again teaching Morse code signals by flashlight at night. The knowledge of Morse signaling was a boon to the village, since we did not have any postal service at that time.

In 1947 a new political party, named the Mizo Union,

was started. Its main aim and object was to secure freedom of the people from the sovereign rule of the maharaja and to form a democratic government. I was chosen as the secretary for the newly created Mizo Union political party volunteers in the Manipur Hills. Since most of my time was devoted to the work of this political organization, I was compelled to resign my post as village schoolteacher-cum-evangelist.

My work with the Mizo Union took me to Imphal, the capital of Manipur State. While there, I was struck with acute rheumatism, which made me bedridden for over two weeks. I felt that I would never recover from my illness. I began to think deeply. Perhaps this was a punishment for the change I had made in my vocation. I was now preaching politics to the people, when the Almighty needed me more! I wept and prayed for forgiveness. "I have sinned. I have turned from you, O God. If only I am delivered from my sickness, I will quit politics to be of service to You forever." My silent prayers were answered. Miraculously, I was healed within a very short time.

The Almighty had delivered me from sickness, and I had promised Him my wholehearted service. I had to come out of politics, but how? If I returned to my village, I would be warmly welcomed and drawn irresistably into politics again. I thought, I want to become a pastor. Because I wanted to enroll in a Bible school, and because that Bible school belonged to the North East India General Mission, I left the Independent Church of India, telling them, "I'm going to Bible school, so I will no longer be an evangelistic teacher."

I decided to go the North East India General Mission Headquarters in Churachandpur, Manipur. I applied to the principal of the mission Bible school for admission. He told me that the instruction would be in the English language. Admission was open only to those who had passed class eight, but I had only passed class six.

I told my story to the principal. I told him that I had been working with a political organization, and that I wanted to change and study the Bible. The principal was moved by my sincerity. He granted me permission to study the Bible for three months. My results in the three-month course examinations would enable the principal to make a fair decision after that. Thus in 1949 I began studies at the trinitarian Bible school.

My results in the three-month Bible study course were surprising. In every subject I earned an honors mark. The principal was convinced. He not only gave me a class eight certificate to avoid objections from other students, but he also admitted me to the full-term course of studies in Bible school in Churachandpur.

Six months later, I was elected monitor of the Bible students studying with me. Besides this honor, I was given some typing work to do in the office.

My three-year Bible study course passed pleasantly, with morning classes and evening classes and Boy Scouts training in between.

Our principal, the Reverend Royal C. Paddock, had come from America. He preached one Sunday morning, but no one translated his message because we were all Bible students who studied in English. There was no need to translate. But one sister, whose name was Thliri, was an uneducated person—she didn't know any English words. After he preached the sermon, she said, "Brother Lerthansung, our principal can speak very well in Hmar."

"No, no, no, he did not speak in Hmar. He spoke in English," I told her.

But she said, "No, no, no, I could understand what he said. He can speak very well in the Hmar language." This was the work of the Holy Spirit.

We had one subject called "Denominations," where we learned that the apostolic church of old had used only the name of Jesus in baptism, according to Acts 2:38. When I heard these things, my heart was greatly impressed. I compared the Scriptures to what was actually being practiced. In the Scriptures, I found that only the name of Jesus was used for baptism and that *baptism* meant *immersion*. In practice, however, the words "Father, Son and Holy Ghost" were being used, and instead of immersion, water was being sprinkled on the forehead of the believer.

My reading and analysis of the Scriptures led me to the principal. One night I went to his house. The principal asked, "What do you want?"

"Principal, I want to talk about baptism. According to our class, in the apostles' time believers took water baptism in Jesus' name, but in the North East India Mission we never call the name of Jesus. We say, 'I baptize you in the name of the Father, Son and Holy Ghost.' So we need to change our doctrine, according to the Bible. In the Bible school we must change our doctrine and go according to the Bible." I told him that according to the Bible we are to be immersed in water, whereas in practice our church sprinkled water. I suggested that the church and the Bible school accept immersion in water and baptize only in the name of Jesus.

The principal responded, "Brother Lerthansung, I am

a principal, but I have no authority to change our doctrine. If we want to change our doctrine, we must put it up to the assembly. Then the assembly will consider. You are a monitor; I am a principal—we have no authority." Having no reply to my rather probing question, he advised me, "Go to the vice principal, because he is an officer in the church administration."

I went to the vice principal and told him the same thing. He told me that thousands and thousands had already been baptized in the name of the Father, Son, and Holy Ghost and were content with the sprinkling of water. Therefore, he advised that I be content with the form and manner likewise.

My own private disagreement with the traditional practice left me thinking. I did not want to carry on a long debate with our most venerable teacher. I only thanked the Almighty when in 1952 I graduated from Bible school. I inwardly longed for someone to baptize me in the manner that I believed to be true and correct according to the Scriptures. At last I informed the principal, "Principal, according to our class, I accept the name of Jesus. Now I am going back to my home. If I can find a capable person who can baptize me in the name of Jesus, I will be baptized in the name of Jesus."

The principal said, "I have no objection. It's up to you."

I left Bible school and came back to my home town. During 1952 I could not find a pastor who would baptize me. Though I had graduated from their Bible college, I didn't want to be sent by that mission. If they could not change their doctrine, I didn't want to work with them.

I had an opportunity to train as a pharmacist. I went

Coming to God

to the medical college at Dibrugarh for training to be a pharmacist and sell medicine. When I completed my nine-month course, just before final examinations we had a holiday. I came back to my home town, wanting to sell some medicine. I invited two people to help. We carried two baskets full of medicine on our shoulders and went to Mizoram in February 1953. From village to village we visited, selling medicine and, whenever possible, preaching to the villagers we met.

In the village of Hlimen, near Aizawl, we stayed about one week. Every night we had discussions on the Bible. It was there that, for the very first time, I had a glimpse of a United Pentecostal Church magazine entitled The *UPC Herald*. It was one page long and was edited by Brother Zakamlova. In one of the articles I read that six people had taken baptism in Jesus' name and two had received the Holy Spirit. The message made a great impact upon my mind. When I read, I exclaimed, "These people took baptism in Jesus' name!" This was the first I'd ever heard of the UPC. When I read, there was great interest in my heart. The magazine stated, "Our headquarters is Mission Bungalow, Adur, Travancore." I wrote down that address.

When I returned to my home village, Senvon, Manipur, I wrote a letter to Brother E. L. Scism, superintendent in India. "Brother E. L. Scism, I want to read your doctrine. If you can send it to me, I'll be happy." I wrote that his article had made a great impression on my mind, and that I needed more UPC doctrine books for my study.

He replied, "We have no UPC doctrine. In the UPC we follow the apostles' doctrine." He very kindly sent me

Lera

three copies of *The Apostles' Doctrine*, a tract written by Brother S. R. Hanby. This engaged my attention for the whole of February, March and April of that year. When I studied the apostles' doctrine, I learned about the one true God. I studied about baptism in Jesus' name and the baptism in the Holy Spirit. This I'd never heard of—baptism in the Holy Spirit. After three months my heart was completely changed.

On April 16, 1953, I wrote a letter to the UPC pastor, explaining my convictions and requesting, "Please come to my house. I want to take baptism in Jesus' name." It appears that my first letter did not arouse the attention of the UPC pastor. I wrote to him again, requesting him to consider baptizing me by immersion and in the name of Jesus. I was delighted to receive his letter telling me that he would be visiting our village in the last week of April 1953.

Pastor Sangkhuma and his friend came from Rawkot to our village. On April 24, 1953, Chawnglienhmang and I were baptized in Jesus' name in a river near Senvon.

Lerthansung visiting his home town for Christmas 1983. Even today, the fastest way to travel the one hundred miles from Lakhipur to Senvon is a five-day boat trip. The forests along the way are full of monkeys and elephants.

Coming to God

The authors at a tender age.

Stanley Scism and Lerthansung Tryte at work on manuscript (December 1986).

Lera

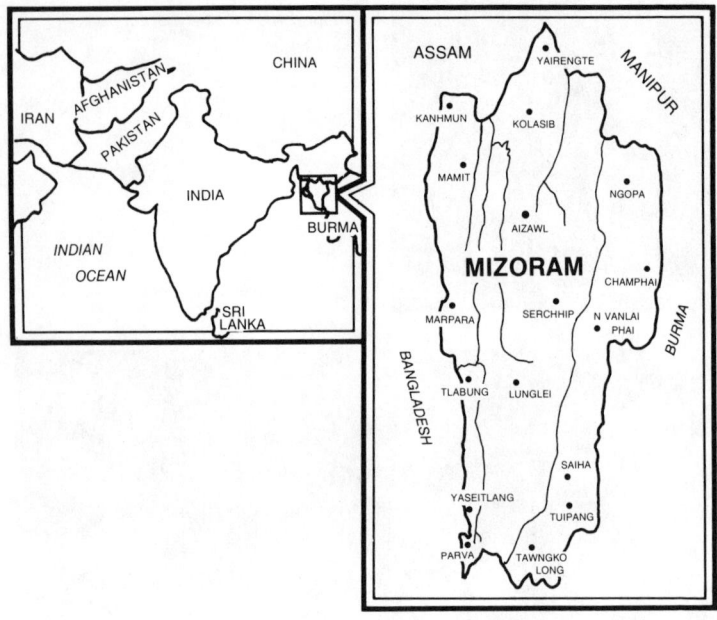

Mizoram

3 (1953-1954)

Spiritual Power

The news of my baptism spread and reached the attention of the pastor of the North East India General Mission. A few days after my baptism, I received a letter from him informing me that since I had taken baptism by immersion in the name of Jesus, I was excommunicated from his church. No longer would I be allowed to preach as a member of the mission church or to hold the position of Sunday school teacher.

I knew that I would be excommunicated from our church and from being a preacher and Sunday school teacher, but inwardly I rejoiced, for I knew that I had to suffer for my convictions. More was yet to come.

That evening, my mother-in-law and my grandparents were very angry. Hearing of my expulsion from the mission and also of my baptism in the name of Jesus, they visited our home. My mother-in-law's anger was like an uncontrollable fire. She was convinced that I had strayed from Christian precepts. She said I was not worthy to be her son-in-law. "Why did you get rebaptized in Jesus' name? If you continue in this, your wife will not stay with you."

I was heartbroken. I said to my wife, "I cannot force you. It's up to you. If you want to separate from me due to the name of Jesus, I cannot object." My mother-in-law took my wife away from me, and she went to her parents' home.

But God touched my wife's heart. She had a discussion with her parents. My wife said to them, "We've been living together for more than ten years. We never fight and we never quarrel. Why do you want to separate me from my husband?" To her father she said, "This is not good."

Then her parents said, "Oh, her husband has already convinced her. We cannot control his wife." They sent her back to my house that same day. Hallelujah! Due to the name of Jesus, I almost lost my wife.

After I took water baptism, many people, when they saw me, asked "Brother Lerthansung, why were you rebaptized in Jesus' name?" Then we would start discussions about the name of Jesus. During 1953 we had no other subject. Wherever I went, I had to tell people about water baptism in Jesus' name. By this time, all the people in my home village were Christian but were greatly opposed to this "new" doctrine.

The church elders and pastors of the Independent Church of India, the North East India General Mission and other missions formed a committee and met together. They reported to the Manipur government, "Brother Lerthansung is an evil spirit. If you do not compel him to go out of Manipur, he will spoil the Manipur Hills."

After they petitioned the Manipur government to

Spiritual Power

have me expelled from the village and state, the Manipur government sent a high official, Mr. Daiho, advisor to the government of Manipur, to Senvon Village. He summoned me to appear before him. "Brother Lerthansung, you must come to my bungalow tomorrow at 10:00 AM. If you have a doctrinal statement and if you have by-laws, please bring a copy."

I went. Mr. Daiho was a Naga and a Christian of the Baptist mission. I entered his bungalow. When he saw me he asked, "Oh, are you Lerthansung?"

"Yes, yes, sir."

"You are very small. See, here is a full basket of reports on you and petitions against you and your religious beliefs. Please show me your doctrine." As he wanted to examine what I believed and intended to preach, I gave him *The Apostles' Doctrine* by S. R. Hanby. He glanced through it. "Oh, you believe in the one true God?"

"Yes, sir."

"Oh, you baptize in Jesus' name?"

"Yes, sir."

"You believe in the baptism of the Holy Spirit?"

"Yes, sir."

"Oh, you believe in healing ministries?"

"Yes, sir."

"You believe in the Second Coming?"

"Yes, sir."

"Then please give me this copy. I like this."

"Yes, sir, you can keep it. I have another."

At that time God touched Mr. Daiho's heart. He felt there was no truth in the allegations launched against me. On the contrary, Mr. Daiho was convinced that I would build a large congregation. "Brother Lerthansung, if you

Lera

can go by this doctrine, you will convince all the Manipur Christians in the future. Don't worry about it. I will pray for you. But before you leave, you must have a cup of tea."

We had a cup of tea. He was very happy, and we parted in a most friendly manner.

That day, other church leaders and pastors had said to the people, "Lerthansung will go to jail," and many of the people thought so as well. But Mr. Daiho was so happy when he read our apostolic doctrine, and when I came out of the bungalow, he congratulated me. From that time on, other Christians never reported me to the government again.

In July 1953 about eight persons desired baptism in the name of Jesus. It was raining heavily, so we went along the river bank with raised umbrellas to shelter us from the rain. Many people came to watch and share in the baptismal service. We sang one song and we prayed.

Just as I finished praying aloud, a very bright light appeared above our heads in the torrential rain. All the people who gathered saw that bright light. Many believed and some even started to flee for fear of what they saw. Most people of the village believed that mysterious, bright light was from Satan; some believed it was from God. There was great confusion among them.

Around Christmas, we gathered to pray and were about to complete our worship service in the church, when suddenly a bird descended on a table in our midst. We had never seen such a bird before. It seemed to have come out of nowhere and was right there before us all. Then it took to the air and disappeared as mysteriously as it had come. Many of us who had gathered for the prayer meeting were filled with a strange feeling—the feeling

Spiritual Power

of the Holy Ghost. Some of the members began to speak in other tongues and also to prophesy.

In March 1954 I went to Aizawl, the capital of Mizoram, to meet the Brother E. L. Scism, superintendent of India. On Sunday morning, as I started for church, I met a man whom I had never known before. I was relatively new to Aizawl and did not know anyone. This brother, whom I met standing in front of me in the church compound, reached out to shake my hand in a warm and friendly manner. I was surprised when he said he would like to pray for me. I consented to his desire. He put his hand on my head and prayed. "Lord, in 1943 you gave me a vision. In that vision I saw three spiritual leaders—the faces of three persons who will lead the lost souls of Manipur State to you. Today I have seen one of them. I praise you for this revelation. As I promised, I shall not tell him when he will die. But, dear Lord, bless him in his ministry. Amen."

This brother asked me if I had come from Manipur. He went on to say that as far back as 1943 he had seen a vision of me among three persons who would lead lost souls to God. On reflection, I remembered that in 1943, when I was aiding my parents in jhum cultivation, doing work as a sweeper at the airfield, and working in the labor corps in Mizoram, I had received a message or a burning desire to devote my life to the service of God. He had chosen me for his work, and I had prayed for strength to do his mission. I was overjoyed with what this strange brother told me. I believed that God had led me into the right church.

At the UPC conference in Aizawl, I witnessed a great number of people singing and rejoicing and praising God as they were filled with the Holy Ghost. All the people were singing in unknown tongues. I had never heard anything like this before. I still did not receive the Holy Ghost, and I prayed to God for this blessing. He told me that in heaven, I would sing a new song. I thought of the many different peoples of the multitude of languages they speak, and of the common language God gives in which to praise Him.

My thinking led me to fear and wonder. I needed the Holy Ghost to enter and fill me so that I, too, could have that common language—the language of God's blessed children. From that day I wanted to have such an experience in the Holy Ghost.

During the conference at Aizawl, I realized that I needed to be filled with the Holy Ghost. Some of the brothers and sisters prayed for me, but nothing seemed to be changed in me. On our way back home, we stayed in a village called Buollon and had a church service that night. During the service, one sister prophesied, "Brother Lerthansung needs to be filled with the Holy Ghost. We all need to pray for him after the service is over." Then some brothers and sisters came and prayed for me. My heart was filled with joy; I was delighted. I wanted to say "Hallelujah" and join them, but I still hesitated to say "Hallelujah" because it was a strange word to me.

The next day we left Buollon Village and proceeded toward Lungsum Village, which is about twelve miles from Buollon. The road zigzags and is narrow. Sometimes we lost the way, because the road is very temporary under the thick forest.

At last we reached Lungsum Village, from which we could see our country, Manipur State. There I stayed in

Spiritual Power

Brother Laltura's house. The believers again prayed for me in the night. It seemed to me as if I had a new tongue, but still I was ashamed and refused to express it.

The next day I went back to my village. I wanted someone to pray with me, but I was the only man in our village who desired to have the Holy Ghost. I longed so much for the people who had prayed for me in Mizoram. Sometimes I prayed toward Mizoram, hoping that they would come. My desire reminded me of Psalm 42:1-3: "As the hart panteth after the water brooks, so panteth my soul after thee, O God. My soul thirsteth for God, for the living God: when shall I come and appear before God? My tears have been my meat day and night, while they continually say unto me, Where is thy God?"

For May 16-18, 1954, we planned to hold the first conference of the Manipur District of the UPC. On Sunday evening I went to the jungle to pray to be filled with the Holy Spirit. While I prayed, I saw a great vision. The Lord showed me what my condition had been during the Mizoram conference. A big basket full of blessings came down from heaven and fell down before me. I did not want to open that basket, so I left it alone. Then a second basket full of blessings came down again from heaven in front of me (representing the prayer at Buollon), but I did not want to open that basket either. A third basket full of blessings came down from heaven again in front of me at Lungsum Village. Once again I refused to open it. The Lord Jesus told me, "I wanted to fill you with my Spirit, but you denied me many times. You have one last chance."

I cried out loudly like Esau, "Hast thou but one blessing, my Lord Jesus? Bless me, even me also." I lifted up my voice to the Lord and wept. Then I came back to the

Lera

house where the saints were worshiping the Lord. I entered with a cry, "I need to be filled with the Holy Ghost. I am needy, I am needy!" I sat down on the bench and cried loudly.

Brother Duoila and Sister Kawlthangpui came and prayed for me. Around 4:00 PM I was baptized with the Holy Ghost and received another great vision. In the vision, I saw my body lying down on the ground. An angel took me beside the heavenly throne, and I sang a new song along with a group of seraphim. We flew together around the throne.

After three hours, I woke up and saw my friends worshiping the Lord with dancing and singing. My mouth was still filled with other tongues and I could not speak properly. All of my people were surprised and exclaimed, "Look, look, Brother Lerthansung is speaking in tongues!" My heart was filled with joy, and my mouth was filled with a new tongue. After refusing the blessing of our Lord Jesus many times, at last I received the Holy Ghost and a great vision for my ministry also.

4 (1954)

Spiritual Preparation

On May 18, 1954, I had heard a voice speak to me, saying, "I have a special plan to train you for My ministry. It will take you about six months to gain wisdom that surpasses human understanding, and you will understand deep things from creatures, hills, waters, birds, flowers, and rain."

I was drawn by the Holy Spirit to a lonely, wooded hilltop overlooking Senvon Village. As I prayed and meditated there in solitude, the Holy Spirit filled me with unspeakable joy. I gazed at the far distant hills of Mizoram. Some were tall, some less tall, and others low. I wanted to ask them, "What is the reason for your being so? If you are high, then all be high together, and if you are low, then be low together."

The hills seemed to respond to my question, "Whether we are tall or less tall or just low, our Creator made us for His purpose. We do not want to change ourselves. From the beginning of time we have remained close to each other. We are content with ourselves. We are not

Lera

jealous of one another, nor do we despise our existence. Our Creator made us silent for His purpose, and His purpose is to reveal His power and glory to those who seek knowledge."

The words of wisdom that the hills seemed to utter filled me with fear and great respect for my Creator. I took out my notebook and started writing down that we must be content and must always be happy as we are. I also found that we must not be jealous or look down upon another person.

After a while, still on that hilltop, I heard the sound of birds chirping on the branches of a nearby tree. As I stood below, I began to think of what the birds were saying and of how, from the very beginning of creation they have chirped in the same manner.

While I was thus thinking, a voice from the birds seemed to say, "Our message is unadulterated from creation till we die. It is the voice our Creator gave us that glorifies His wisdom, His power, and His creation. We don't have power to change our way of chirping. We chirp according to the way God made us, and we are very happy with it. We don't want to change it. Why have you people not used the same language God gave you in the Garden of Eden instead of following the wrong path and taking the way Satan likes?"

Then I realized that we people have lost much of the likeness we had to God in Eden. The chirping of the birds taught me a great deal on how to talk. Sometimes the mouth from which we speak good words also speaks evil words. The birds teach us to speak only truth. Everything we speak should be the way God wants it, yet since his fall in Eden, man has seldom used his voice to praise his

Spiritual Preparation

Creator.

Below the hill on which I was standing a large river flowed ceaselessly onward. I looked at the river and thought, River, you are flowing forever onward. You always seem to be in a great hurry. Your murmuring, rushing, roaring voice seems to have a message for me. Tell me what truth you hide from man.

The waters of the river seemed to reply, "Like all God's creation, we are rushing recklessly toward our destination. For us that destination is the far-off ocean. As we travel along, we carry with us whatever comes in our path. When we reach the great ocean, our rushing and roaring are lost in the noise of the great ocean waves. We are no more ourselves but part of that mighty ocean."

I reflected on the message of the river. Yes, we are all moving irresistibly onward toward a destination. In our ceaseless movement to reach it we gather with us many things that are all lost in the mighty ocean of eternity. Of this ocean there is no end, and once there we shall say no more goodbyes. How great and magnificent is our Creator! Then there will be no more tribes or races. We shall all be part of the body of Jesus Christ. Sorrow will be no more. What a day of rejoicing that will be!

Some distance away I saw some flowers. What message would they have for me? The leaves of the flowering tree were green. Its petals were tinged with red and white. It looked so beautiful, so simple, so true. I asked the flowers to tell me their secret and the simple purity of their existence.

The flowers seemed to respond, "We are dressed in our Creator's purity and love for us. He made us silent in our existence. The beauty and fragrance we impart to those who look at us compel the sensitive soul to know His purity, His fragrance, and His great mind."

I reflected on the message of the flowers. Truly we have departed from His purity and His love. We have tried to clothe ourselves against His order. Our worship, too, must be pure, simple, and true. The flowers taught me that we must stay true to the gospel of Christ and must try to be the light of the world.

One day I went to our jhum to work. Near where I was working was a cucumber plant with fruit on it. I wanted to eat one, but just before I plucked it, a snake came crawling over and rested on that cucumber. Then the Holy Spirit within me spoke out in another tongue. I realized that the message in tongues was a rebuking of the snake. Without stopping, I spoke in tongues. After a while, the snake lifted up half of its body and fell flat on the ground, dead. Then I laughed aloud, saying, "Speaking in tongues is a real gift of the Holy Ghost. Even snakes cannot stand against it. God has given the true believers power to speak out life and death." This reminded me of God's power when He struck Ananias and Sapphira. How great is His deliverance for those who trust in God!

God gave me new songs in my mouth to sing to Him. Since I didn't have any friends to sing along with, I used to feel very lonely. One night while I was lying in bed, a heavy rain came. The frogs were croaking peacefully together at the playground. When I heard their sound, it was already midnight and still raining heavily. I got up from my bed and went to the playground to join the frogs. It was very dark and the place was very muddy, but the sound I heard was melodious to my ears. I sat

Spiritual Preparation

down on that muddy ground and I started singing the new songs that the Holy Ghost had given me. Along with the frogs, I started praising God in the playground. I wanted to stay with them the whole night, but lest my family should worry, I left the playground about three o'clock in the morning.

Three days later I went to the river to fish. Fishing was not my main aim; instead I wanted to join the river in making loud noises as it flowed along. In one spot a strong current made a louder noise. I sat on one of the big rocks nearby and said, "River, I came to join you as you praise the Lord. Let us praise the God who created us." I happily joined the river, singing with it and praising God for almost four hours.

The rivers have taught me many deep meanings. The rivers say to me, "We cannot stop in one day. We must flow every night and day to the ocean with a beautiful noise. You also must not stop in this world before you reach your destination in heaven. Make noise for the Lord God. Praise Him."

I went back home again. The flowing rivers, the frogs in the ponds—these I found praising God their Creator more than most believers do. I found that all created things are real messengers of God.

One day in June 1954, I went to the forest to pray. While I was walking, rain starting pouring and thunder and lightning continued for an hour. I felt very lonely and I wept. Along with the thunder and lightning, I prayed and gave praise to God sitting on His throne. I felt as though I joined and accompanied Him. After giving long praise to the Lord, I felt as if I were landing back on earth. From then on I realized that even lightning and thunder are instruments for praising God. Those who hear the thunder's sound with their physical ears may be afraid, but those who hear it with their spiritual ears know that it is praise to the Lord. From that time on I have never exalted silent prayer, for I know that God wants a great sound in worshiping Him.

After I praised the Lord with the thunder and lightning, the Holy Spirit guided me to an understanding of rain. It seems that there are two kinds of rain—special rain and ordinary rain. Special rain is necessary for vegetables and trees and flowers, so we need not pray for it to stop. Instead, we must try to find a place of shelter. But if it is necessary for the rain to stop in order for people to have a meeting or a worship service, they can pray to God that the ordinary rain will stop until the service is over. On the Lake of Galilee, Jesus commanded the ordinary rains and storms to be silent.

After completing my spiritual training, one night I went to the river bank to pray. While I was praying, Satan appeared to me in a vision in the form of big vulture. He was as big as a buffalo, and he charged me. We had a fierce battle. God gave me the sharp sword of Michael, and with the help of that sword, I cut off the left wing of Satan's form. Consequently, he went away, but before he disappeared he turned back and said, "I will come again someday and fight you again." With that he left.

I shouted back at him, "In the name of Jesus, I'm not scared of you."

In 1962 and 1963 the devil came back twice to fight me, but the Lord was always with me and I always defeated him. From that first battle I realized that victory only comes from God. The Holy Ghost within us is

Spiritual Preparation

more powerful than Satan. If we use Jesus' name as our fort, Satan will in no way defeat us. God gave me this knowledge through the Holy Ghost. Since then, God has led me to different people, large and small, to teach them His wonderful message.

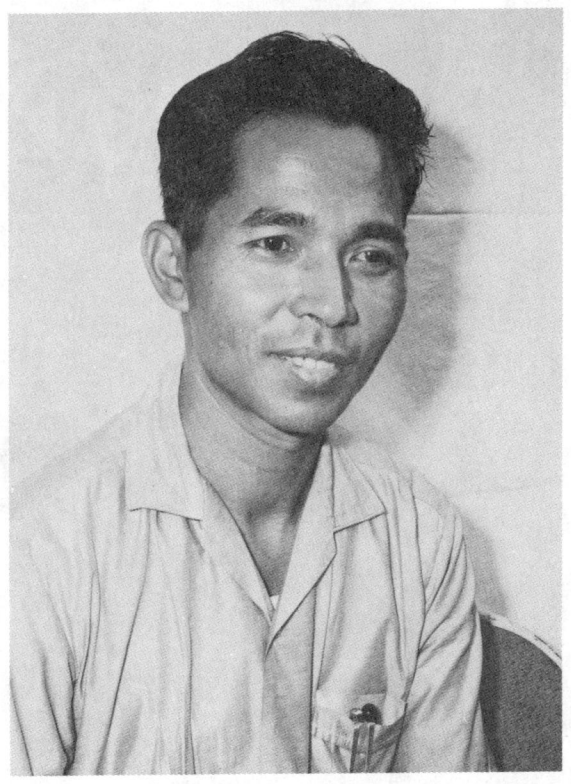

The young Lerthansung (1950s).

Lera

Lerthansung and his wife, Darchawng, in December 1986.

5 (1954-1957)
Senvon, Manipur

In 1954 I became district secretary of Manipur. There was no other capable person. There were only 150 people and two churches in the district.

[Small founding memberships, few workers and great distances in terms of travel time—these and other factors contributed to the decision to form districts as early as possible, E. L. Scism points out. And he adds, "Besides, for district secretary you need someone with a little business acumen," an ability Lerthansung had demonstrated in his sales journeys to Burma. In India, the harvest is so great and the laborers so few that E. L. Scism and Harry Scism moved people into areas of responsibility as soon as possible, and although there are always some disappointments, most of the young men blossomed under the encouragement, the appreciation, and especially the trust. These men have borne, and continue to bear, much fruit.]

When I was district secretary I was not paid as a full-time worker, but I had no time for any other work. I

Lera

received ten rupees (about seventy-five cents) per month. We never thought of finances; we were so happy to have found true doctrine.

[Remembering financial support back then, E. L. Scism remarks, "Those days were kinda tough on all of us."]

Later in 1954 a boy named Lalnghet, who was about five years old, died suddenly about eight o'clock in the morning. His grandparents were cultivating a field about six miles from home. Some young men went to inform them, but they weren't able to get back home until about twelve noon.

While the boy's body was laid on his bed and people were digging his grave and making a coffin, we UPC believers heard about the death and went to the boy's home. I felt the power of the Holy Ghost within me. The Spirit led me to tell those who had gathered there, "Since the people of Senvon do not accept or believe in the power of the Holy Ghost we will pray. The boy who is dead will respond to our songs of praise, but he will die immediately thereafter."

I asked Brother Hminga to pray. While those gathered began to sing and pray with spiritual songs, the boy started moving his hand and began saying, "Hallelujah." Everyone saw the movements of his hand and heard him and knew that the child was not dead. But immediately after our prayers, the boy died again, signifying that true life comes only in Jesus. Because of that great miracle, many started believing in the work of the Holy Spirit. However, some people said it was the work of an evil spirit.

When we tried to construct a UPC church at Senvon

Senvon, Manipur

Village, Lunkhopao, the village chief, said, "You cannot build a UPC church in Senvon." I replied that under the Indian constitution we were at liberty to build a church wherever we wished and to propagate our religion freely. He said that he would report the matter to the authorities, and I replied that he was most welcome to do so. Later, the Senvon chief took another step of opposition to our building program. He said that he would not allow any material from Senvon Village or from the forests nearby to be used for the construction of the church. All the other churches could take material from the forest freely.

We started collecting money among us, saying, "We shall buy the material elsewhere, but we will have our church built." Our firm and unflinching desire to construct a UPC building in Senvon Village in the face of day-to-day opposition further kindled the flame to get the job done at all costs. Church members and others voluntarily came forward with offerings, and the building materials denied to us by the chief of the village and his supporters were purchased and brought in from outside. Today the UPC building at Senvon stands as a noteworthy achievement of an ardent and determined group of people to propagate their beliefs to all.

Pastor Sangkhum conducted the opening service of our church at Senvon, and something unique happened. One of our evangelists, Brother Chawnglienhmang, was asked to preach in tongues. He gave a prophetic message. Although it was unintelligible to the rest of the people, the Holy Spirit within me gave the interpretation.

Every word that he prophesied was significant. I could understand the depth and intensity of his prophecy.

When I interpreted that prophecy, some believed and accepted; others could not believe. The prophecy has been proven by now, for many things have been fulfilled as interpreted.

After our church service, we sang and worshiped the Lord with rejoicing and dancing. One of the ladies was baptized with the Holy Ghost and began to speak in tongues. Her brother was greatly displeased with her; when they returned home he beat her severely. She later said that she felt no pain at all. A few days later, her brother was afflicted with swelling on his hands and arms. He feared death. He requested us to pray for his forgiveness and thereafter became an ardent member of the church.

Since we had new believers who received the Holy Spirit, we had prayer together in a house every night. Since we made a great noise, non-Pentecostal people who did not believe in our new experience also could not tolerate our noise. Some young men came and burned chilies under the house in an attempt to stop our prayer meeting. Sometimes we could not continue our prayer service due to the intense burning sensation in the air. But after some years, God touched the hearts of the people who tried to make us suffer, and they became members of the UPC. Then they gave interesting testimonies.

In 1954, unfortunately our first district pastor fell into sin and starting smoking. Our superintendent, Brother E. L. Scism, wrote to him. "Since you can't stop your smoking, you cannot be a pastor," and he dropped his license. On March 1, 1955, I was appointed district pastor (presbyter) for the Manipur District, under the leadership of Brother E. L. Scism, superintendent of India, at the

Aizawl conference. I gladly started my pastoral work.

In those days, there were no vehicles, so all journeys had to be made on foot, and we had to carry our own bedding. In some villages the villagers would say that if a person was a member of the UPC, he couldn't sleep properly in a house. But we didn't mind; we gladly slept under trees or on verandas. Sometimes we couldn't sleep well in those places because there were many rats, frogs, leeches, and mosquitoes.

The road, from Senvon to Aizawl, about 140 miles long, is dangerous since wild animals like tigers and elephants roam freely. In the rainy season we encounter many leeches which suck our blood, but we bear it all happily for the name of Jesus.

Once I was retuning from Aizawl to Senvon, and I came to a big river called the Tuivai. Since it was already late, I spent the night at the river bank, sleeping on top of a big rock. While I was lying on the rock, a big tiger came near me and moved about the whole night. That tiger stayed near the rock the whole night, and left me in the morning. No mosquitoes came around me that night but went to the tiger instead. I realized that God had sent the tiger to guard me so that no other animals would harm me. In the morning I gave thanks to the Lord for giving me a good guard. That day I reached our village safely. If we are in Him, all things belong to us in the name of Jesus.

In May 1955 I went from Senvon up to Churachandpur to preach the full gospel. The distance is over 130 miles. After spending four nights in transit, I reached my destination. On the way, I had to pass many villages. Some villages paid attention to what I preached to them, but some villages did not allow me to spend the night and kicked me out of their village. All the church leaders said that I was a messenger of an evil spirit.

After three days I reached the mission headquarters in Churachandpur where I had graduated from Bible school. I put up at the house of H. L. Sela, the general treasurer of the mission. My old friends and the head of the mission church came to me that very night and asked, "Why did you go to the United Pentecostal Church after graduating from our Bible school? Tell us the reason why you turned away from our doctrine."

I replied to them that the mission believed in the trinity, but since I could not find the trinity written in the Bible, I believed in one God only. Moreover, they baptized by saying "in the name of the Father, Son and Holy Spirit," but in the Bible I found that we should take water baptism in the name of the Lord Jesus for the remission of our sins according to Acts 2:38. Since I alone could not convert the whole mission to believe in one God, if I remained under the mission, I would have no chance to preach about the one true God and Jesus Name baptism in Northeast India. Therefore I decided to find an organization that believed in one true God. If I did, I decided I would join it. Fortunately, I had found the UPC, and now I was planning to build a UPC church in Churachandpur and lead all the members of the mission to believe in the one true God.

Hearing this, the leaders of the mission became very angry. They summoned ten pastors and had a debate with me. On that great day the Lord was at my side. Their most senior pastor stood up and said, "Since Lerthansung is standing on the Word of God, the questions he puts to us cannot be answered. Since we do not stand on the Word of God, it is impossible to defeat him." With that we concluded the discussion.

From then on, many people started paying attention to the UPC. On the other hand, the trinitarians gave orders to the people not to pay attention when I preached the gospel. They said that I believed in false doctrine. Still, many people who were baptized by the Holy Ghost invited me into their houses and gave me a good opportunity to preach the gospel there.

In this way I was able to preach in different villages, and many people were baptized in the name of Jesus. Some people who wanted to receive the Holy Spirit went into the mountains. There we prayed for them, and they received the Holy Ghost. With the help of God, the UPC was established in four villages during that time.

In June 1955 I went from Senvon to Churachandpur. On the way, in a place called Kailantlang (range of Kailam), the hills were thickly forested and full of fog. A heavy rain fell down from early morning on. We did not have an umbrella, so we cut some big leaves of a banana tree to cover ourselves. The way was full of leeches. I told my friends not to bother over three to five leeches and that unless they came up with more than twenty leeches on their legs we must go on to our destination. By evening, we reached Phaipheng Village, which had more than thirty houses.

We asked the house owners, "May we put up in your house for the night?" The answer in every house was no; there was no room for us. We were so cold that our teeth chattered and we could not talk properly.

There was a big house in the center of the village.

Lera

I told my friends to put down their luggage and to begin to pray. We bowed down on the ground and prayed to the Lord. After several minutes, the house owner came to me and said, "Tonight you can put up in my house, so do not worry. While you were praying to God, my heart was filled with love for you." Then we put up in his house safely.

Just before we left the next day, I gave the house owner a shirt as a token of appreciation. He was so happy and promised me, "When you return, I will welcome you again." I realized that prayer can make a great change.

By 1956 more than five hundred people had taken water baptism in the name of Jesus, and we had four churches and eight preaching points.

In March 1957 I went to Mizoram for a conference, and after we finished our conference, I headed back home. On the way is a village called Melriat, where lived a lady named Lalnunmawii who suffered from tuberculosis. She was admitted to Durtland Presbyterian Church Hospital, but the doctor had given up hope and told her family to remove her from the hospital as she was going to die soon.

We were having an open-air meeting in the village. While I was preaching, the lady was listening from her house. After our service, she sent a man to call me to pray for her. Just before I went Brother Zakamlova, the district pastor, told me, "See, Pastor Lerthansung, that sister is suffering from tuberculosis. If you go and pray for her, do not stand in front of her but stand at the back." After he told me this, I went to Lalnunmawii's house, went near her, stood in front of her, and started to pray for her. I was very touched when I saw her great desire to be healed. I felt great pity and love for her. My tears flowed uncontrollably, and she also cried.

Just as we finished praying, she told me that she wanted to be baptized in the name of Jesus but asked how we could do it since she could not walk alone. I called one of our pastors, Lalbiakthanga, to help me. Holding her hands on both sides, we went down to the river. I offered a prayer to God, then told her, "Sister, I want to tell you not only that baptism in the name of Jesus is for the remission of our sins, but also that Jesus died for our infirmities. Today you must bury not only your sins, but also your TB." With that, I baptized her in the name of Jesus.

As she came out from the water, she cried out happily, "I am healed, I am healed! God has healed me. I will be able to go home alone without any helper." And she did.

That evening we had dinner in her house. After dinner we went to the church building. When we entered, she cried out loudly, "I know the name of Jesus. It is the name of my God. I will not be ashamed," and she worshiped the Lord with dancing.

After three days, the Durtland Presbyterian Church Hospital doctor who had released her heard about the news and wanted to check her. Twice she took X-rays of Sister Lalnunmawii, but she found that all the TB had disappeared. The doctor confirmed that Sister Lalnunmawii was completely healed, but she did not believe that it was due to her taking water baptism. The doctor had come from London, England, as a missionary to Mizoram.

Pastor Kappu of Senvon belonged to the Assemblies of God. He used to pray, "God, don't give me the Spirit and spiritual songs like Pastor Lerthansung and the UPC, but give me the real Holy Ghost and the real spiritual song

Lera

from the third heaven." One day he saw a great vision from above, and from that experience he realized that he needed to obey the Bible and be baptized in the name of Jesus for the remission of sins. He asked me to baptize him, and I did.

Lerthansung and Vawma entering New Churachandpur, Manipur Hills (November 1956)

6 (1957-1960)
Churachandpur, Manipur

While I was living in Senvon Village, Brother E. L. Scism advised us that the district presbyter should reside in the district headquarters. Since we were increasing rapidly by the help of God, the district conference resolved that "the district headquarters will be shifted to Churachandpur, because that is the headquarters of the government also and the place is central for South Manipur."

In September 1957 my family, along with five friends who helped us carry our bedding and other things, left Senvon Village for Churachandpur. The distance was about 130 miles, and the road went up and down. As there was no transport, we had to walk about fifteen miles a day, six nights and five days, in the jungle. My eldest son, Dinga, could walk by himself, but my second son, Sanga, could not. I carried him on my shoulders and sometimes on my back. Our youngest daughter, Dari, was carried by her mother. After three days of walking up and down, our legs started hurting. We did not have proper food to

Lera

eat—no curry. We started having stomach trouble and all became very exhausted. We had only rice, and all my children wanted curry. But in the jungle there was no curry. What could we do?

On the river bank we made a small hut in which to rest for the night. After we finished our dinner and the family went to bed, I went down to the river to bathe and to pray. After my bath, I knelt down and prayed, "Lord, now we are going to Churachandpur, but my children have no curry and they are complaining to us. Now what to do? You supplied birds to the Israelites in the wilderness. We also need your supply."

After I finished my prayer, I heard a great sound in the river. At first I thought it was a big python, but when I looked around I couldn't see one. The sound seemed to be coming from the water. When I looked carefully, I saw small fish gathering in large numbers near the bank, trying to lay eggs, as is their custom. I quickly ran to my friends, calling, "Please come, please come! I just saw a great feast. God has given us a large number of fish, so we must go down to the river and get them." Carrying our big baskets and pots, we hurried back to the river and easily caught about twelve kilograms altogether. All through our journey we were able to eat proper food, like the Israelites in the wilderness. All the way to Churachandpur we had good curry. I told my children, "This is the supply of God."

As we proceeded on, my daughter kept having serious stomach trouble from dysentery. There was no medicine to give her, so I started praying to God while carrying a cupful of water in my hand. After I finished praying, I gave the water to my daughter, and she was completely healed immediately. Then we continued toward our destination.

When we reached the bus station, none of my children had ever seen a motor vehicle before. They started crying, "Father, we will die. What should we do?" When they saw the bus, they feared it so much.

I told them, "No, you need not fear. We must enter the bus. Then we can go." When we entered and when the bus started going, they almost died with fright.

Just before we reached Churachandpur, a small man named Lienthang came to meet us. He said, "Are you the UPC pastor who is going to Churachandpur?"

I said to him, "Yes, yes. What do you want?"

He continued, "The Lord sent me, saying that there would be a pastor coming from Senvon, moving to Churachandpur, and that I must welcome him. This the Lord told me, but He did not tell me your name. So for that reason I asked you. Brother, did you ever speak to an animal in other tongues? Have you spoken to a deer?"

I replied, "I haven't spoken to a deer!"

He questioned further, "Have you ever spoken at any time to any animal in other tongues?"

I related to him that I had rebuked a snake by speaking in tongues and that the snake died immediately. "God used my tongue to kill the snake."

Upon hearing this, the man went back to his village and his friends and reported our conversation. "Brother Lerthansung is a capable spiritual pastor," he concluded.

After reaching Churachandpur, we rented a small house. The roof was straw and the floor was mud. We lay some straw on the floor and used that for sleeping, as we did not have a bed. When it rained, water entered from the floor, especially at night. Earthworms started coming out from the earth and frogs hopped to our bedding in search of a warm place. It reminded me of the days of Pharaoh. Sometimes my children were afraid of the earthworms and the frogs and asked me to go back to our house in Senvon Village. I told them, "Children, we have no house in our village. We gave our house to the church, and now they have built a big church building in place of our house."

My house at Senvon Village had been in a central place, so the members of our church had requested me to hand over my place to use as the site of the church. I handed it over without taking a single *paisa* (one hundreth of a rupee). The thought came to me that when we needed a personal house, God would consider us. From that time even until today, we have had no personal house or permanent address. When I retire, where I will go I do not know, but I trust in Him and expect a heavenly home.

At that time we had no members in Churachandpur. I wrote a letter and made it into a pamphlet, which said, "I have come as a UPC pastor from Senvon Village. Those who want to receive the Holy Spirit can come to my house every evening. Those who want to learn about the Bible I will freely teach." I distributed this to every village and every home. In October, November, and December of 1957 I opened a Bible school. We taught doctrine and surveyed the Bible from Genesis to Revelation. We had four subjects. This Bible school was very successful. After we closed it, half the students took baptism in Jesus' name, thirty-six of them. Brother Sawivela, now the Churachandpur pastor, was one of those first students.

Churachandpur, Manipur

Meanwhile, every night people came to our house to receive the Holy Spirit. We prayed and they received the Holy Spirit. After a short while, we were able to have a big church in Churachandpur by the help of God.

On New Year's Day 1960, while having our morning food, my wife informed me that there was no more rice to cook for the evening and told me to buy some. But when I opened our savings box there was no money left. I told her, "Beloved wife, we prayed to Him in 1959 and asked God to supply the daily food for our family, and for the whole year God gave us our daily food. I just realized that in this new year, 1960, we need to ask God again to give us our daily food for the year. Let us all pray to God to give us our evening meal." Then we closed the doors and all started to pray. When we finished our prayer we heard a knock on the door.

Jamedar Chalthianga was standing there. He asked, "Pastor, how are you?"

"We are all right by the help of God. What do you want?"

"This morning I heard the voice of God while in prayer. He told me not to give my tithe to the Presbyterian church to which I belong, but to those who work for the Lord and for the lost souls. I did not know who He meant, but the Lord Jesus told me to go to your house. Now I am giving you my tithe, ten rupees. I've never done this sort of thing before. This is my first time."

"Brother Chalthianga, you are doing the right thing. See, we have no more food to eat even for this evening, nor do we have any money to buy food. But God listened to our prayer and answered us through you." Happily I accepted the ten rupees and was thus able to buy our evening food. All our family and Brother Jamedar Chalthianga again gathered together and offered our thanks to God because He had answered our prayer. Back then we could purchase about twenty-six kilograms of rice with ten rupees. Praise the Lord! It reminded me of the manna from God in the wilderness.

By February 16 prices of all commodities had risen rapidly. The monthly help I received from our mission was just enough to buy rice only. There was no money left to buy mustard oil to fry the curry. Therefore we would not be able to take food properly, without which I knew our health would go down. Then a thought came to me; The Bible says that whatever we need we should tell our Heavenly Father, and He will provide for us. Remembering that Bible verse, I called my family together and told them that we would have to pray to God. "Lord, in order that we may be able to do Your work efficiently we need to have healthy bodies. So, Lord, please give us oil to make our curry," we prayed. After one hour we finished praying.

Two women from Saipum Village came to my house about that time and asked, "Pastor, how are you?"

"We are all right by the help of God. Please come inside." They came in and sat down.

One of them told me, "Pastor, yesterday we killed our pigs, but we did not have time to invite you. My husband and I felt bad to have food without your family to join the feast. Now my husband told me to give you three kilograms of pig oil and some pork. We have come to your house for this purpose."

I then explained, "Just before you arrived, we prayed for God to give us oil. Now God has answered our prayer

Churachandpur, Manipur

through you." Generally we hill people use pig oil to make curry. We all happily offered our thanks to God together, and I have never forgotten what God told us: "Ask, and it shall be given" (Matthew 7:7).

I invited Brother E. L. Scism, superintendent of India, to come to Churachandpur to open our new church and also to attend our district conference. In 1960 I received some funds for this, and on March 3 I met him at Imphal Airport and met his smiling face.

There was no good hotel in Churachandpur, so he stayed in a small house used as a shop. There was no cook, no bathroom, and no partitions—just one room. I became cook and sweeper for him. I made roti (flat bread) for him, cut it in pieces, and mixed it with eggs. He ate it happily.

Since there was no latrine, I took an empty tin (similar to a five-gallon kerosene can) and covered it with some small wooden planks in which I had cut a hole. It was very simple, but he was happy. Every morning I went to his room and emptied it. When Brother E. L. Scism came, I was the district pastor, cook, and toilet cleaner. He told me to get another person to do this, but I replied, "While you are in my district, I will take personal responsibility for everything." I was really happy and content.

[Brother E. L. Scism remembers that while he stayed at this house, Brother Lerthansung's nephew used to sleep at the house at night. Every evening the nephew would say, "I have to answer the call of nature," and would promptly disappear. From the same house he once saw and photographed a monkey riding on a pig's back, going down the street.]

Since there had been no white man for many years in Manipur, many people came to the church to see a big white man. After hearing his messages, thirteen people were baptized in the name of Jesus.

At that time Brother Satinvela, who is now the superintendent of Northeast India, also took water baptism in Jesus' name. His family became so angry that they refused to give him his monthly school tuition fee.

I encouraged him. "Brother Satinvela, you need not worry. I will write a letter to Brother Harry Scism."

Brother Harry Scism loved Brother Satinvela very much. He was very kind and promised, "I will help on Brother Satinvela's tuition fee." He helped him until graduation, and Brother Satinvela finished high school by the loving kindness of our Brother Harry E. Scism. After Brother Satinvela graduated, I sent him to the UPC Bible school in Kerala.

In 1960 at Churachandpur, Brother Lamzakhup, who was the chief of Saipum Village, walked about seven miles to attend a communion service. His father was lying in bed and almost dead. He told me, "Pastor, I need to take the Lord's Supper for my father, because I heard that God has performed miracles during the Lord's Supper." As he took the Lord's Supper, his father who was lying at home was completely healed. The next night they came together to our church and gave their testimony.

Another interesting event happened near Churachandpur at a later time. In September 1977 several pastors and I planned a crusade in Tongkham Village, and we started by foot from Churachandpur. The monsoons had begun, and to get to Tongkham we had to travel through a dense forest path. Despite the inclement weather, nothing could stop us from leaving our village and traveling to Tongkham. We set out early in the morning, and the rains beat down mercilessly upon us. Leeches got into our shoes, and our umbrellas were of little use; but we continued our trek. Toward evening, a thick, heavy fog engulfed the whole forest area, but we continued walking. We soon realized that we had lost our way.

Presently, we saw a village ahead of us in the distance. Villagers came to meet us and asked us where we intended to go and what our mission was. We told them that we had planned a crusade and that we were preachers going towards Tongkham Village. They told us that we were far from Tongkham Village and that we were in Bungjang Village. We had completely lost our way. The villagers were good to us, and after we had dried our drenched clothing, we began to tell them about the one true God and baptism in the name of Jesus. They told us that, although they were Christians, they had never heard the true gospel as we had told it to them. They requested us to stay several days in the village. Many were convinced by our message and were baptized, and the UPC was established in that village.

In the Book of Acts Paul and Silas went to preach the gospel in Galatia and the Spirit of Jesus led them to Macedonia to preach the gospel and convert people there. In the same way we, too, felt that God wanted us to go to Bungjang Village to establish His true church. Thanks be to the Lord!

Lera

The first Bible students at the seminar Lerthansung conducted to bring new people to the Oneness truth (1957). After the seminar half of these accepted the truth and joined the church.

Lerthansung and E. L. Scism when the latter visited India in 1973.

7 (1959-1963)
East Manipur

[This chapter begins a new phase of Lerthansung's work. Now, only six years after his baptism, his ministry began making major inroads into new territory—new languages, new geographic areas, new cultures and customs. During this period he proved himself capable and qualified to become later the missions director for all of Northeast India.]

In November 1959, I invited Brother D. K. Biswas to come up for a revival in the Churachandpur area. At six places we held revival meetings, and we took those who needed to receive the baptism of the Holy Spirit into the jungle. We arranged a good spot for the prayer meetings. Sometimes there were four to six hundred people; sometimes even seven hundred or over one thousand went to the jungle. We requested them to sit properly; then we explained to them how the Holy Spirit moves. We requested all the people to raise their hands and say, "Hallelujah."

When we prayed for the Holy Spirit, the Spirit came

Lera

upon some like a great storm and a fire. Many people fell down. The Holy Spirit was manifested in many ways, and some people saw great visions and received prophecies. Many received the Spirit and spoke in tongues.

After praying, we asked for testimonies. Many people testified, "When we prayed together and when we said, 'Hallelujah, hallelujah,' a great fire came near me. I couldn't tolerate it; it was very hot. I fell to the ground."

Then we explained, "The Holy Spirit came as a fire to this area."

Some people from East Manipur, members of the Anal (pronounced "uh-null") tribe, came to our revival meetings in the Churachandpur area and received the Holy Ghost. These people were mostly associated with the American Baptists. When they went back to their homes, they invited Brother D. K. Biswas to have revival meetings there, and many people received the Holy Ghost.

I told Brother Biswas, "If they received the Holy Spirit, then they need to take water baptism in Jesus' name."

Brother Biswas refused. "No, no, no. This time we don't need to say anything about water baptism—only about the baptism in the Holy Spirit. This is our first step."

But the church leaders of the Baptist mission, when they heard of this, were very angry. They could not do anything to me because I was from Manipur, but against Brother Biswas they complained to the government, "He came from Calcutta; he spoiled our church." This was convenient for me, for after Brother Biswas left, the church people wanted me to visit every month. So I took advantage of the opportunity. I went to Chakpikarong myself.

East Manipur

The Revival people (Spirit-filled people) there wanted to know more of the truth, but I could not speak their language. Since I could not speak Manipuri, what was I to do? I cannot speak Manipuri, but if there is some person who can translate my sermon, that will be good, I thought. There was no suitable person there at first, but fortunately a man named Heldong came from Manipur to Chakpikarong. He could speak very well in Manipuri, and he knew my mother tongue, Hmar, very well.

The first night we had our meeting and while we were praying together, one man prayed very loudly in Mizo. (The Mizo language, formerly known as Lushai, is the most widely used language among the tribal hill people.) The man spoke clearly, and I was so happy. Oh, here is a man who speaks Mizo; I can preach in Mizo and he can translate, I thought. After the prayer meeting, I went to him. His name was Ngamtun and the people called him a prophet. "Brother, chibai, chibai," I told him, which means, "Greetings." He did not know *chibai;* he did not know a single word. I told him, "While you prayed to God, you spoke in Mizo very loudly. For that reason I wanted to say, 'Chibai.'"

He replied, "No, no, no, I never spoke in Mizo. I do not know Mizo. The Holy Spirit gave me a new tongue, so I prayed to God in unknown tongues."

Then the thought came to me, Ah, this is the work of the Holy Spirit, the same work as occurred on the Day of Pentecost. This was my first experience to hear someone speak in tongues in a language I knew.

When I was called to preach the sermon, Brother Heldong translated into Manipuri, and the people understood very well. We presented the Word of God.

Lera

I taught them about the one true God and about baptism in the name of Jesus. "Brothers and sisters, you already received the Holy Spirit. This is very good, but the Holy Spirit baptism is only part of the new birth. If we want to go to heaven, we need to be born of both water and Spirit. Since you are already born of the Holy Spirit, you now need to be born of the water. Previously you have been taught simply water baptism by immersion in the name of the Father, Son and Holy Ghost. But please open your Bibles to Acts 2:38."

When they saw that Peter had told the people to take water baptism in Jesus' name, they felt no need for discussion. They all changed their minds when they compared my words to the Bible. They came to realize the truth from the Bible, so they told me that since they now *knew* the right way, they wanted to *follow* the right way. "Hmmm. We already received the Holy Spirit. We need to take water baptism in Jesus' name."

After the church meeting, we went to the Chakpi River. It was very, very big. I told them, "First I'm going into the water. Then, after I pray, you can come one by one." When I entered into the water, I prayed to the Lord. After my prayer, they came one by one and I baptized them. The water was very deep. When I had baptized them in Jesus' name, the people did not want to come out of the water afterward.

We started at noon and continued until two o'clock. In those two hours, 450 people took baptism. For one place at one time, this is my greatest record—the most I have ever baptized in one day. Having received the Holy Ghost, they were led into the truth.

Although they had taken water baptism in Jesus'

East Manipur

name, they did not join the UPC. They stayed with the Apostolic Free Church. I told them, "I cannot compel you. I cannot force you to come to the UPC. First of all I want to present the truth." I held services in more than twelve villages, and at every one we presented the gospel truth.

A young man named S. R. Tourngam received the Holy Spirit. I told the people, "If you have a young man who wants to go to Bible school, I will recommend him to our Bible school in Adur, Kerala."

They were happy. "Yes, we have such a young man, Brother Tourngam. He is studying in class eight. If you recommend him, we shall be happy."

Brother Tourngam came before me for an interview. We spoke together in English. At that time, he could not speak well in English—only a little and that was hopeless. Nevertheless I recommended him for the Adur Bible school under Brother E. L. Scism, and he went.

After he graduated, he convinced the people to join the UPC. They agreed, "Oh, we need to join the UPC. If we stand alone, we are a small group. Better to join." When Brother Harry Scism came to Hmarkolien in Cachar District, they sent some delegates from East Manipur. Then they affiliated with the UPC and became the East Manipur District of the UPC. They had fifteen hundred believers. Brother Scism requested me to visit there with Brother Damhuala to open the new field, so we went and established the new district.

At one baptismal meeting there, some pastors of other groups came to listen to what we said. They tried to find false teaching in us. The next day, four pastors came to our office, bringing a big Bible, and those pastors challenged me. "Pastor Lerthansung, we want to challenge you to a debate. We must discuss the one true God and baptism in Jesus' name."

I did not want to invite other people to such a debate. If these pastors say something wrong, that is not so good, I thought. We had a lengthy discussion. I announced, "Brothers, if we are going to have a discussion, I do not want to hear anything beyond the Bible. If we *stay* inside the Bible, we must *say* inside the Bible. I do not want to hear a word outside the Bible, so please open your Bible and according to your Bible you must talk to me."

Then we started on the subject of the one true God. After talking for an hour, they could not say anything. They believed in the one true God. "If we want to become true Christians, then we need to believe according to the Bible," they confessed.

"Yes, yes. I do not invite you to become UPC, but I invite you to accept the truth," I replied.

Then we started another subject—baptism in Jesus' name. I asked one question. "Could you please show me in the Bible where they took water baptism in the name of the Father, Son and Holy Ghost? Please show me." When they opened the Bible, they could not find it. After talking for one hour, they accepted baptism in Jesus' name also.

At last the four pastors asked, "If we want to take water baptism right now, can we do it?"

"Yes, yes. There is no fixed time in the Bible. Whenever you want to take water baptism, that is the right time. Philip and the eunuch went together on the road. The eunuch accepted the truth like you, then they went to the water and he took water baptism. The jailer took water baptism in the nighttime. Therefore, for water baptism there is no fixed time."

"We are willing to take water baptism, but if we are among other people we will be a little ashamed because we are pastors. So please let us go to the river now."

We went to the river. We had no spare clothes, but there were no strangers there, so I instructed, "Just take your clothes off. No need to be ashamed. No women here."

Later that day I told the people, "The four pastors took water baptism," but they didn't believe me, so that night I made and distributed to the four pastors their baptismal certificates. When this happened, the people were so happy that they laughed and laughed.

This is the only time I baptized four pastors at once although I baptized three pastors at one time in Bangladesh. Sometimes I repeat to the people, "I am a small figure, but if we speak real truth, God will bless us. The Lord is working with us. Other pastors may be very big, but through Jesus we can convert them."

The East Manipur people had a great burden for the Kuki people. Between Kohima and Imphal is a big town in the Kuki area. In March 1963 some believers of the Anal tribe and I hired a bus and traveled there. Then we went to Kangpokpi Village on the northern side of Manipur. This town was the headquarters of the American Baptist Mission in Manipur.

When the political leaders heard that we were going to Kangpokpi Village, they sent a message: "Brother Lerthansung is a Hmar. He troubled our headquarters in Chakpikarong. If he comes, you need not give him any chance to preach." Not only that, they sent another message to the police: "When Brother Lerthansung

Lera

comes, please keep him in custody. If he preaches anything, he will spoil our Kangpokpi church."

Some people of the Kuki tribe had invited us to preach the full gospel and about the baptism in the Holy Ghost. When leaders of the Baptist mission heard about our plans for Kangpokpi, they also informed the police station: "Reverend Lerthansung and his party are coming over here, so do not give them any chances to preach in the church. If you do, trouble will come, so don't even let them stay in Kangpokpi Village."

On the way to Kangpokpi, forty-two people came with me from East Manipur. All the way they sang in Manipuri. When we reached the village, we began meetings in a house.

The Holy Spirit came on us, and thirty people were filled. As they received, some fell on the ground and started speaking in other tongues and could not get up for a long time. At that moment, the police officer came in and looked at us all. He called me over and asked, "Pastor, those people lying on the ground—will they be able to sober up again? What will happen to them?"

I told him, "These people are receiving the Holy Spirit according to the Bible. They will be all right again. They will leave their past sins. Those who were thieves will no longer be. Those who drank liquor will no longer drink after they have received this experience." I further told him that the police wouldn't have much work in regard to these people.

The police officers came and watched and listened to our preaching. When they heard our message, they did not find any mistakes.

After a while, those people who had been lying on the

East Manipur

ground stood up and became very happy. They started saying, "Hallelujah! Praise the Lord!" and confessing their own sins before the Lord.

The police were very happy. The officer took me to the police station, and we had a nice cup of tea. He explained, "See, the Baptist church sent a report telling us not to give you a chance to preach, but I like very much the way you preach about the full gospel and about the Holy Spirit. Why is this? How is it?"

"Those Baptist church leaders do not understand many Bible verses properly. We came to help them see what is right. They were scared their members would join us. To prevent that, they sent you this report."

Over thirty people wanted to take water baptism, so the next morning we went to Run River for a baptismal service. When I first entered into the water, I prayed to the Lord and dedicated the water.

[This is the usual practice in Northeast India. This very serious attitude toward baptism, this willingness to spend time, energy and prayer on it, has brought such concentration of faith that many people have been healed as a result of baptism in the powerful name of Jesus.]

After I prayed, people started coming down one by one to be baptized. Among them was a girl called Miss Veizachin. She was in class nine at that time. She was a beautiful girl. As soon as she came and sat in the water, she started weeping. Sometimes she shouted very nicely, but she could not stop weeping. After I baptized her in Jesus' name, she did not want to come out of the water. She cried, "Lord, I am so happy, I am so happy, I am so happy." She kept crying and saying, "I am so happy."

After the baptismal service, I went to her. She still

could not stop her crying. At last I told her, "Sister, please stop crying, in the name of Jesus. Get up." I took her by the hand and she stopped crying and stood up. "Sister, you say, 'I am very happy, I am very happy,' but you are crying and crying. This is contradictory. What is the matter?"

"Oh, pastor, while you were in the water and prayed, I saw heaven open. Suddenly a very big bridge came down from heaven to the river. From that bridge, countless angels came down and stood with you all the time during the service. I felt so happy when I saw the great throne, and I wanted to climb up that bridge and go to that place, but the angel would not permit me and said, 'It is not time to come up here. Later you will come.' When I saw heaven, I was so happy, but I couldn't go. For that reason I am crying."

A minute later, as we started from the river, two Naga women came and without saying anything stepped into the water. They could not understand my language, but I went back to the river and baptized them in Jesus' name.

Shortly afterward, they gave their testimony. "From very far we watched your service. From heaven a bridge came down and many white ducks also came down. They filled up the water and when you said, 'Hallelujah,' more came from heaven. One told us, 'This is the good way. If you want to go to heaven, you must take water baptism in Jesus' name.' We believed that this baptism is from God and that we needed it, too."

Those two women were Buonkulu and Khumai of the Naga tribe. I have never heard such names or forgotten theirs.

After the service was over, we went home happily. It was the first baptismal service in that area, so we could not explain much to the people, but God ordained the service in the sight of the people and blessed it. Many people were also healed from their sicknesses. That time also we had great success.

Unfortunately, a man called Himan went to Chakpikarong and taught about the Sabbath. Many people started observing the Sabbath again. I told them, "If you teach everyone to observe the Sabbath, you cannot become part of the UPC. In the UPC we don't observe the Sabbath." To date they still teach that everyone should keep the Sabbath. For that reason in that area we have no preaching points. We presented the full gospel, but we could not include them in the UPC.

Brother Himan said, "I saw a vision. The Lord said, 'Since you have received the Holy Spirit and taken water baptism, that's very good. Now you need to observe the Sabbath. This teaching is very important for the Christian.'" So he prophesied to the people. The people heard him and said, "It may be true." They followed Brother Himan. Though they received the Holy Spirit and took water baptism, we cannot include them in our organization.

This is the work of the East Manipur District.

Lera

Pastor Lerthansung baptizing at Hmarkolien, Cachar District (1965).

Praying to dedicate the water at a baptismal service.

UPC boat being dedicated at Hmarkolien (1965).

8 (1961-1964)
Cachar

During 1961 I received a letter from Rinenga of the Assam police in Silchar, Cachar District, Assam State. He had seen my name in the UPC *Herald,* and he now invited me to visit Cachar District to preach the gospel. "We want to hear the apostolic doctrine. If you can come, we want to hear."

At that time I had no money, so as soon as I received the letter, I informed the church people. "The Cachar people have called me like the Macedonian call, but I have no money. If you can give, then I can visit."

Then Brother Zama, a photographer, stood up. "If you want to go to Cachar, I will go with you and will pay our fares from Manipur to Cachar." At that time airfare from Imphal, Manipur, to Silchar, Cacher, was only twenty-two rupees. That night, I received one hundred rupees. I flew to Cachar.

After I landed in Silchar, I had to go by bus, since the place where we were to have our services was a little far. We reached Paloi Village and stayed three days.

Lera

Every night we had service and preached the full gospel. Our message was new to them, for they belonged to the Presbyterian church.

After three days we had a baptismal service in Paloi Village, and six persons were baptized in Jesus' name. Then I left Paloi Village for Hmarkolien Village, where I had studied high school for a short time. We visited Hmarkolien from house to house. Another church had scheduled revival meetings in Jairawm Village, so some friends invited me to go there. We walked about fifteen miles to Jairawm Village, but I did not have a chance to preach in the church. However, my friends arranged an open-air meeting, which gave me a good opportunity to preach the gospel in Jairawm Village.

After the meetings there, some of my friends had a great desire for the Holy Ghost. They secretly requested me to have prayer for them in the jungle so that they could receive the Holy Ghost. One brother and one sister received the Holy Ghost, speaking with other tongues. After hearing about this new experience, more people wanted me to have prayer meetings for the Holy Spirit.

Unexpectedly, Lunzagin, a church elder of Jorkha Village Presbyterian Church, invited me to his village. We walked there about six miles. When we reached Jorkha, the villagers and church elders desired to have the Holy Ghost. They told me, "If we receive the Holy Spirit from your ministry, we shall leave our Presbyterian church."

After hearing our message, forty-five people went along with me into the jungle to pray for the Holy Ghost. At the first prayer meeting, about thirty-six people were baptized with the Holy Ghost and spoke in other tongues as He gave utterance. Some people prophesied and some received interpretations from the Holy Spirit.

One Sunday morning we had a baptismal service at the Jiri River, and about fifty-four people took water baptism in the name of Jesus. Instantly, they affiliated with the UPC along with all the members of their churches.

The next week we went to Jirimukh Village and continued our revival meetings there. All the members of the church took water baptism in the name of Jesus, received the baptism of the Holy Ghost, and then affiliated with the UPC as had Jorkha Village. They dropped all their bad habits like smoking, chewing betel nut and drinking.

[The closest thing to chewing betel nut in the West is probably chewing tobacco. Chewing betel nut is habit-forming, and it turns the mouth a vivid red.]

During our revival meetings, no people went to the shop to purchase cigarettes or betel nut. One day the shopkeeper called me. "Pastor, did you give them orders not to purchase cigarettes or betel nut from my shop?"

"No, I cannot give such an order to them. It's only that they received the Holy Ghost during our revival meetings, and this made them stop such bad habits."

The shopkeeper responded, "If so, there is no profit for me here, so I will close my shop and move to another village. The people told me, 'We were professing Christians before Pastor Lerthansung arrived here, but now after receiving the Holy Ghost we have become true Christians. We the Jirimukh Christians no longer need any more cigarettes or other bad habits.'" So he left.

One meeting I particularly remember. After our baptismal service, we wanted to have the Lord's Supper also, so we made arrangements. I invited the village chief to

Lera

attend our church. He answered, "I cannot tolerate your UPC meetings. I don't enjoy them."

I told him, "No, no, no, we are going to have the Lord's Supper. At our Lord's Supper, God blesses us so much. Those who want to be healed from their bodily sicknesses can be healed during the Lord's Supper. For the Lord's Supper, the Lord ordained bread and fruit of the vine to represent His body and blood. Those who have faith in Him can be healed in their bodies if they take the bread and wine. Jesus ordained the Lord's Supper for our body and our spirit. Jesus is the healer, Jehovah-Raphah. One woman suffered an issue of blood. She touched his clothes and was completely healed. Jesus Himself touched blind men, and they were healed. So Jesus is our healer; He can heal our body and He can heal our spirit." When he heard these things, the chief attended our church.

At the church, I explained about the bread and wine. "The bread we must take instead of His body, the wine instead of His blood." After we explained about the Lord's Supper, the chief prayed and partook.

He had been suffering from backaches. After he prayed, he stood up and exclaimed, "Oh, my backbone is completely healed! I am so happy! Tomorrow I will take water baptism in Jesus' name."

This was the first Lord's Supper and baptismal service in Cachar. From that time the Cachar work has continued to progress. Each year I visited Cachar many times, since at that time I was district pastor for both Manipur and Cachar.

I went to Hmarkolien Village another time to preach the full gospel, and we had a baptismal service. A man named Lianhmingthanga, director emeritus of the Indo-

Burma Pioneer Mission of the Cachar District, had a long discussion and a great debate with me. At first he was very angry because I had baptized his granddaughters. He asked me to write down the scriptural references for our teaching on baptism. I wrote them down and gave them to him.

After one week he called me again to his residence. "Lerthansung, I wanted to criticize and condemn you concerning baptism in the name of Jesus, but I find after reading my Scofield Bible and my commentaries that you are quite right. So I want to be baptized in the name of Jesus, but what can I do? I have been suffering from malaria fever every day and have been shivering."

"If you don't mind, I will call a rickshaw to carry you to the river. Pastor Lianhmingthanga, your malaria fever must also be buried along with your sins." I baptized him in the name of Jesus.

When he came out of the water, he said, "I am completely healed of malaria fever." He was seventy-nine years old.

His last words to me were, "I want to rebaptize in the name of Jesus the thousands of people whom I baptized the wrong way. Lord, forgive me, forgive me." He was a faithful member of the UPC up to his last day.

Over the years I have baptized more than twenty pastors who despised me at first and spoke evil words against me. But after they heard the truth, God turned them to the truth. Though they were pastors and had baptized many people, they did not want to remain without remission for their sins, so they came to be baptized in Jesus' name.

In 1962 I made plans for Bible seminars in Cachar.

Lera

I needed to take my typewriter along with me for the Bible seminar. In April I went to Imphal, the capital of Manipur. When I booked my luggage at the air office the booking clerk told me that I needed to give him eight rupees for excess luggage. I did not have any extra money in my pocket. I said to the booking clerk, "Please wait a few minutes. I need to meet my friend at Tribal Colony."

I went to Tribal Colony to the residence of Brother Ngunchunga. He was about to go to his office, but I told him, "Brother Ngunchunga, I need eight rupees for my excess luggage in the air office. I have no other money, so we need to pray urgently." We both prayed to God and asked for eight rupees.

Just after we prayed, Brother Thangkhuma came by bicycle to our place. He cried out, "Brother Ngunchunga, I want to meet Reverend Lerthansung before he leaves Imphal. I want to give him twenty rupees for his ministry." He gave twenty rupees. I went back to the air office, booked my luggage, and went to the airport by bus.

Just before we left the city a customs officer came to the bus and said, "I want to see Reverend Lerthansung." Many people sitting in the bus believed that I was a smuggler, but the customs officer gave me forty rupees. He is a faithful member of the UPC.

Just before I entered in the security room at the airport, Brother Ngunchunga, who had prayed with me, came by jeep to the airport and met me. "Brother, this morning we drew our monthly pay. Now I want to give you forty rupees for your ministry in Cachar District." So that time I received more money than I asked God for. Hallelujah!

9 (1963)
Divine Protection

> *"If it had not been the LORD who was on our side, when men rose up against us: then they had swallowed us up quick, when their wrath was kindled against us. . . .Our help is in the name of the LORD, who made heaven and earth"* (Psalm 124:2-3, 8).

The greatest example of divine protection in my ministry occurred on October 1, 1963, at my birthplace. We had a conference and an open-air meeting there and preached about baptism in Jesus' name. From Silchar to my home town we had to go by boat. The journey took about four days and four nights. People from Mizoram and from Manipur came also. I preached about Jesus' name. "Brothers and sisters, our mother churches here in Manipur are the North East Indian General Mission and the Independent Church. When they take water baptism, they say, 'I baptize you,' but they never baptize. They sprinkle. *Baptize* means *immerse*. If they say, 'I bap-

Lera

tize you,' then they should immerse, but they never immerse; they just sprinkle some water. This is a great mistake in the sight of God and in the sight of the people."

After I said these things, three people in the village formed a committee and confronted me. "Pastor Lerthansung, you blame us in front of the people. What should we do?" They also tried to force their young people to take action. "If you do not kill Brother Lerthansung, he will spoil our church." At our church meeting, where more than one thousand people had gathered together, they called me to stand in the middle of the people, and the leader asked, "Why, Brother Lerthansung, did you blame the other church pastors? We are so angry. This is very bad."

"Sir, I never blamed other pastors, but I explained about water baptism. I never mentioned the name of your pastors. I explained that baptism means immersion, not sprinkling, but I never blamed your pastors. I don't even know who they are."

That night we had great trouble, but after this discussion, half of the people loved me. The other part wanted to kill me. Some village authorities said to each other, "If we do not separate the people, they will start fighting. Half the people love Lerthansung; half the people want to kill him. It is not so good." The authorities interrupted the meeting. "Brothers and sisters, please keep quiet, please keep quiet," they insisted, so we had to keep quiet.

On that visit more then thirty people took water baptism. Some of my friends had no hope that I would come out alive, but thanks to God I escaped from great danger of death. Now sometimes I tell young preachers, "When we meet with trouble during our ministry, this is the real

Divine Protection

test. We cannot let opposition stop us from doing something. If we cannot tolerate danger and persecution, if we fear these things, then we cannot be successful. We will not harvest spiritual fruit. In this I have some experience."

After Senvon, we went to the Vangai range and had an open-air meeting in the village of Patpuihmun. There we had no UPC members. The people wanted to hear our message and requested us to have an open-air meeting. We had one, and thousands and thousands of people gathered together. But one brother was very angry while I was preaching the gospel. "Brother Lerthansung, we do not want to hear about baptism in Jesus' name! We do not want to hear about baptism in the Holy Spirit! Please stop! Please stop!" Then he started throwing stones. Fortunately, he did not hit me, but he hit three other persons, and they were so angry that they wanted to kill him.

Some other people told us that they would not allow us to preach about the baptism with the Holy Ghost and furthermore told us to get out of their village. They even stoned us, but a man named Rozama, who had a desire to receive the Holy Ghost, invited me to preach in his house. "If there is trouble in the open-air meeting, please come to my house. I will have authority in my house, and you will not have trouble."

"Oh, brothers and all the people, those who want to hear more messages from Brother Lerthansung can come to my house. I will open my house for the preaching," Brother Rozama informed the people. We moved to his house, and the whole night we discussed doctrine. Some young men wanted to make trouble, but Brother Rozama is a very strong man. "You cannot say anything. This is my house," he said. Thus God delivered me from that terrible stoning.

In that village at least eleven took water baptism. They requested me to stay longer, and we started a church building.

It is very easy to make such a building. We obtained building materials from the jungle. The girls carried bamboo, and the young men carried wooden posts. In one week we completed the church building. We used sun grass and bamboo, and in one week we finished.

The next day we traveled to a village named Ankhasuo on the bank of the Barak River named Ankhasuo. The villagers all belonged to the Independent Church of India, but they wanted to hear our message.

We had meetings in a house, and every night more and more people came. The church leaders and village authorities formed a committee to stop us.

On the night of October 17 before our evening service, I received a strong warning letter. "Brother Lerthansung, you have no UPC members here, and you are like a wolf putting on a sheepskin. You spoil our church. If you stay, surely we will have division and separation in our church. You need to go on October 18. If you do not leave tomorrow, we will kill you and bury you here." Some people had signed the letter, so I went to the jungle and prayed for them.

They had also informed other villages, "If Brother Lerthansung does not leave our village at once, we shall kill him." As a result many people came from many villages to find out if I had been killed or not. Many people came, wanting to hear our message. So this was a big

Divine Protection

conference, and we liked that. That night, we had a great meeting.

I told the people, "Brothers and sisters, I received a strong letter from your village authorities and church leaders. If I do not leave tomorrow, they want to kill me. But one thing we must do: if you already know the truth and if you want to obey the Word of God, all those who want to take water baptism in Jesus' name can do so tomorrow morning. If you do not take water baptism in the name of Jesus, I will leave this village."

On October 18, thirty-seven people took water baptism. These were important men—politicians and shopkeepers.

Then the committee said, If we kill him, these people will stand behind him. What shall we do? That night about 1:00 AM, the first of the people who had signed their names to that letter came and knocked on the door.

When I went to open it, my host said, "Pastor, please do not go out. I want to welcome them and see who they are."

When he opened the door, the pastor of the Independent church came to my room and apologized. "Pastor, I want to make an apology. Please forgive me, please forgive me. I was chairman of the committee that wrote the letter, but my church members forced me. For that reason I had to give my signature. Please forgive me, please forgive me."

I responded, "Pastor, you need not make an apology. When I received your letter, I prayed to the Lord, so you need not be troubled. God will forgive you if you repent."

As he had come, secretly he went out. That same night all the people who gave signatures came secretly and gave

Lera

apologies. Now we have a big church in that village in Manipur.

I left that village on October 20 and reached another village. There we had an open-air meeting. One pastor, who had been my teacher while I studied the ABCs in 1933, scolded me. "Brother Lerthansung, if you do not leave this village tonight, it will be a sad thing for you."

I replied, "If you are not the landlord of this village, you have no authority to compel me to leave. Please tell me. Are you the landlord or not?"

"I am a pastor but not a landlord." That very night he went away from that village because the people were very eager to hear our message. The next day several headmen of the village and schoolteachers took water baptism in the name of Jesus.

District Pastor Lerthansung preaches at the Cachar District conference (1967). K. L. Hnuna is seated at lower right.

10 (1964)

Cachar II

After I came back to the district headquarters in Manipur in 1964, I went to the Jiribam area in Cachar District and preached about our full gospel. That was Pastor Sehkholam's jurisdiction. At that time he was a Baptist Mission pastor. I did not know him, but he heard about my visit to his area. He was so angry. He made up an order, sent it to every village, and gave me a copy. "Brother Lerthansung is an evil spirit. His doctrine is false doctrine. If he comes back to Jiribam area, you need not give him a cup of water. You need not talk to him."

When I read his order, I decided to reply. I wrote, "Brother Sehkholam, I received your order. I want to ask some questions. Please answer. There are two doctrines—the Nicene doctrine and the apostles' doctrine. Please tell me which doctrine you are following. If you believe the Nicene doctrine, you will believe in the trinity; if you believe the apostles' doctrine, you will believe in the one true God. If you believe the Nicene doctrine, you will baptize in the name of Father, Son and Holy Ghost; if you

Lera

follow the apostles' doctrine, you will baptize in the name of Jesus."

After one week he wrote a letter to me. "Brother Lerthansung, I received your letter. Come to my book room. We must have a discussion. I have invited twenty-seven church elders and theologians. If we defeat you, you need not come back to Jiribam. If you defeat us, we are going to take water baptism."

I went to Jiribam. From Lakhipur to Jiribam is about ten miles. I took a taxi. The twenty-seven church elders and Brother Sehkholam and his wife were sitting together, and they had arranged a chair for me.

When I entered I told them "Brothers and sisters, according to our custom, if we want to discuss a marriage we need to take a cup of tea. Now I am going to invite you to become part of the bride of Christ, so I will pay the price. Please order tea and cake from the hotel. I will pay." They went to the hotel and bought cups of tea and some bread, and I gave the money. They were so happy.

"Thanks to Brother Lerthansung we can eat some nice bread and have a nice cup of tea," they said.

When I heard this I thought, Oh, if they are so happy, then I will start. I started to speak about the one true God, and baptism in Jesus' name, and I did not want to stop. I continued for about one hour.

Finally Brother Sehkholam stood up. "Brother Lerthansung, we need not discuss any longer. You stand in the Bible; we stand outside the Bible. So we cannot have a discussion. Better to go to the river."

That day twenty-seven church elders and Pastor Sehkholam and his wife took baptism in Jesus' name. When church leaders take water baptism in Jesus' name,

Cachar II

then other people realize the truth also. By converting the leaders, we can convert the people. This is the work of God.

That day I wanted to return to Lakhipur. Brother Sehkholam saw me off at the bus station. When I entered into the bus, Brother Sehkholam said, "Brother Lerthansung, please shake hands, please shake hands." When I touched his hand, he cried loudly, "Long before, I hated you so much, but today I'm looking for you, looking for you."

Some of the people and the village authorities were very angry and had ideas to do bad things to me. They called me into the village court and asked me to explain points they could not understand. I explained, "We the UPC have already registered with the government, so I have a right to preach everywhere." (Paul used a similar tactic in Philippi.) Then the village authorities changed their minds, and many people took water baptism in the name of Jesus. Now that village is our sectional headquarters.

In 1964 we had a conference in Fullertol. Brother E. L. Scism came to Silchar.

[Brother Scism remembers staying in the Dak Bungalow in Lakhipur. He thinks it might be at this time that he gave a bicycle and a typewriter to Brother Lerthansung, who had done a great deal before he received anything from America.]

The people appealed to have separate districts. Brother E. L. Scism said, "This is good. Now we have more than one thousand members in Cachar, so they need to have a separate district. Since we have no capable person in Cachar to be district pastor, Brother Lerthansung

Lera

needs to come to Cachar. Then we shall have an election in Manipur to replace Brother Lerthansung."

This was resolved, so I was appointed as district pastor and Brother T. R. Khama as district secretary-treasurer. Since 1962 I had been working as district presbyter for both Manipur and Cachar, but from April 1964 I began working as district presbyter for Cachar only, and Hmarkolien became the headquarters for the Cachar District of the UPC.

At the next district conference in Manipur, we elected for district pastor Brother T. R. Challian, and I handed everything to him. We had a great farewell meeting at Churachandpur, where I delivered a farewell address to the people. "We are but strangers in this world, and according to the Great Commission of our Lord Jesus, we must go into the whole world. We cannot stay in one place. In doing the work of God, we must continually go forward until we reach heaven. Our spirit is like flowing water. Water never rests but flows day and night until it reaches its destination in the ocean. We in the UPC also cannot take rest until we reach our destination—heaven. If God wills, I will go forward from Cachar District also." We sang a farewell song and ended with a closing prayer.

During my ministry in Manipur from 1955 to August 1964, God gave me fifteen churches and several preaching points. I baptized fifteen hundred people, and more than one thousand received the Holy Ghost.

After a great farewell, our family flew from Manipur to Cachar on September 17, 1964. Brother Kawra and some sisters came to the airfield to meet us. From the airfield we went straight to Hmarkolien and arrived safely.

The people there had arranged an old house for our family. The floor swung, and in some places there was a danger of falling down under the house. The walls were made out of bamboo and so was the floor. The roof was sun grass, and the veranda was made out of logs. When we went out, it was necessary to be careful because there were some holes between the logs. But the Holy Spirit moved in with us, and we never cared about our house's condition.

In October 1964 we had a baptismal service at Hmarkolien Village. More than one thousand people gathered together to see an immersion baptism in the name of Jesus, which they had never seen. We prayed to God just before I went down to the water. Suddenly, some people heard a great storm coming, and the water formed great waves. The spectators were afraid of the great storm and ran away. As for us, we could not feel the wind or storm, and everything remained the same. On that day fourteen people took water baptism and seven people were baptized with the Holy Ghost.

When we got back to our headquarters, the people asked, "How could you stand on the river bank that evening when you had the baptismal service? A great storm came and we could not stay. We were afraid. That's why we returned. We didn't know what was going on. How could you stand there?" When they realized we didn't know about the storm, then the people of Cachar District said, "Ah, this is a miracle from God," and knew that the Lord was working with us.

God has frequently performed miracles at our baptismal services in various areas over the years. There was

Lera

an old man, aged seventy-nine, at Chandikhal Village who could not walk straight. He was bent over and was only as tall as a small child. We had a baptismal service at the Sakhi River in April 1964. That old man came down to the river and took baptism in the name of Jesus. After his baptism he was able to walk straight like a young man, and he received the baptism of the Holy Ghost. He walked straight up to his last day.

A brother in Chandikhal had rheumatism in one leg and had not been able to wear a shoe on that foot for a long time. He would buy a pair of shoes and just use one shoe. He came to the river and was baptized in the name of Jesus. As he came out of the water he cried, "I am healed! I am healed!" That evening he was able to put on both shoes and still can even today.

Sister Karhliri, aged thirty-eight, was suffering from leprosy in her hand. She had consulted many doctors, but she had received no help at all. She learned that we were going to have a baptismal service at Range River, so she came to the river. After we prayed to God, she washed her leprous hand. God completely healed her. The next morning she came early to my house and told me that she wanted to be baptized in the name of Jesus. It is great to know that God can work miracles for us at water baptism—not only providing remission of our sins but also cleansing us from other things as well. I have received many testimonies from members of our churches who said they buried smoking, drinking, cinema and other bad habits when they were baptized.

11 (1967)
Tripura

The work progressed. In 1967 Brother Damhuala told me, "Brother Lerthansung, we need to go to Tripura State. This is our responsibility." On December 5, we flew from Silchar to Agartala, the capital of Tripura. This was our first visit to Tripura, and we did not know whom we should contact. We simply flew. When we landed in Agartala, we drove and drove and finally put up in the house of an army man, not UPC, whom we knew. He had come from Manipur.

He asked, "What shall we do here since you have come to Agartala? We want to hear your message." The next day we had a meeting in the center for the Assam Rifles.

Our friend contacted the New Zealand Baptist Mission, but their missionary refused us. "Oh, the United Pentecostal Church—we cannot let them preach in our church."

But that day we convinced their headmaster, and he told us, "Brother Lerthansung, though you cannot preach

Lera

in our church, I will give you our high school boardinghouse. I will tell all the high school students to attend that morning if you preach the gospel." So we had service two times in the New Zealand Baptist Mission school boardinghouse. We were very happy.

The Assam Rifles in Agartala also requested us twice to preach the gospel, and three days later, a businessman named Vankhuma Darlong invited us to Darchawi Village to preach.

Brother Damhuala and I told him, "We want to come; we want to come."

The whole night we traveled by truck. There was no good bus, just a full truck. We were in it the whole night.

In the early morning we reached Darchawi Village. Brother Vankhuma introduced us to the pastor and other church leaders. "These pastors came from Lakhipur. They are UPC pastors."

The church leaders said, "Ah, they will preach sermons. One each. After hearing their messages, we shall consider whether we shall continue meetings or not."

First I preached a sermon. The second one Brother Damhuala preached. Our sermons took the whole day. The people were so happy, and they requested us to stay one week more. Every night we had church meetings, and after church we had Bible discussions for which I was responsible.

At that time a missionary who had come from New Zealand and who knew the Mizo language very well came every night to our Bible discussion. That missionary invited us to take a cup of tea. He told me frankly, "Brother, though I am a missionary, I am not a theologian. My father was a missionary. After he died, they appointed

Tripura

me as a missionary. I never went to Bible school. So I'm very interested when you have messages. It is a privilege for me." He was very happy.

All the people welcomed us greatly as the people of Iconium and Lystra welcomed Paul and Barnabas. We preached one last time about the one true God and baptism in Jesus' name. The ladies took a collection for our fare. We received Rs 160 and went back to Lakhipur.

I then left Lakhipur for Mizoram. By the end of the month, and during my absence, many people in Darchawi decided to follow our full gospel. Some of their representatives came to Lakhipur to take water baptism in the name of Jesus. About seven of them were baptized in Hmarkolien.

When they went back home, they wanted to start the UPC there. They convinced some people, then invited me to come back. "We are interested in baptism in Jesus' name. Some people want to take water baptism. Please come down to Tripura."

This time I visited Tripura alone. When the New Zealand Baptist leaders heard that many people were going to take water baptism in the name of Jesus and that the UPC was going to be established in Tripura, they started leading the people against me, as the religious leaders did to Paul and Barnabas in Acts.

When I reached Darchawi, that first night more than three hundred people surrounded the house where I was staying. With swords and spears guns, sticks, fire, they shouted, "Go out tonight; go out from this village. You shall not have any baptismal service today or tomorrow." The whole night they roamed and shouted. Some people wanted to enter the house, but Brother Vankhuma said,

Lera

"If you enter into my house without my permission, I will report you to the police station."

Some of them came inside the house, but I told them frankly, "I want to go away according to your command, but I did not come in my own will. Some people want to take baptism in Jesus' name. How can I leave before I give these people a baptismal service? If you want me to depart, you must convince the people who want to take water baptism. If they do not want to, then I need not stay in this village. If you can convince them, I will leave tomorrow."

Those who wanted to take water baptism declared, "If you want to kill us, kill us. No harm. But first we want to take water baptism."

I stated, "Unless and until I baptize these people, I will not go out from this village."

There was great panic, and great trouble among the people, but by the help of God there were no further disturbances. The next day we had a good baptismal service, and that night we formed the UPC in that area. I informed our opponents, "Since the UPC is recognized by the central government of India, no one can do anything against it."

All the people went back to their homes. By the help of God, the UPC was established in Tripura State. Since we are following the footsteps of the apostles, wherever we go people may think we have come to disturb them, but in the end they realize the truth. It reminded me of how people said in Paul's day that he had turned the world upside down.

After a year we sent Brother Thangchuanga there. After a year he came back. Then we formed a new district,

Tripura

and Brother Damhuala and Brother Harry Scism appointed Brother Ruata as district presbyter for Tripura. Brother Ruata also suffered greatly. They tried to stop our work, but it is still going on.

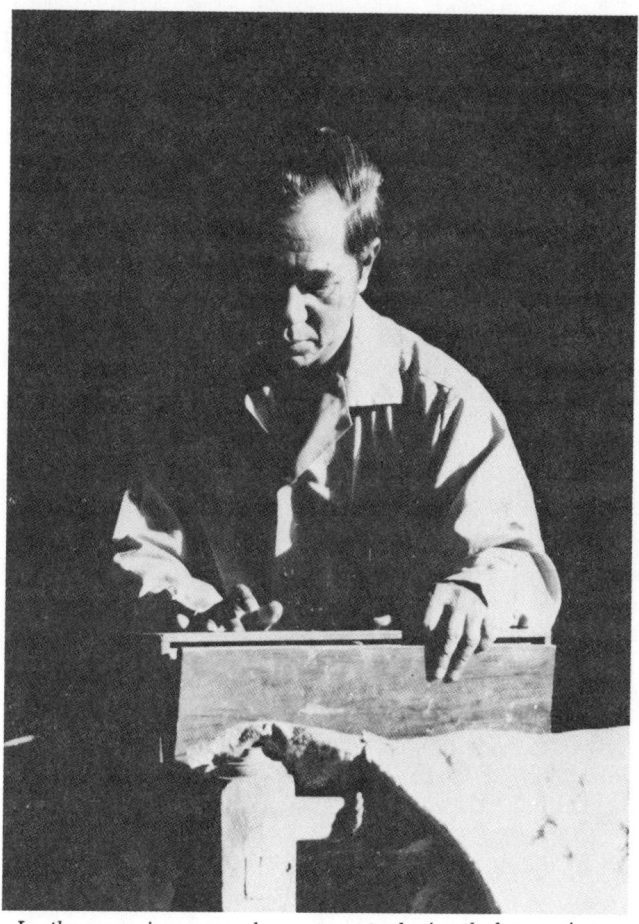

Lerthansung, in a rare solemn moment, playing the harmonium.

12 (1967)
North Cachar Hills

In March 1967 we sent Brother Lalhmudik from the Cachar District conference to Haflong, capital of the North Cachar Hills Assam State. When he reached Haflong, the trinitarian church leaders falsely charged Lalhmudik and reported him to the government. The police put him in jail and sent a telegram to me. "Your pastor is in jail. Please come soon." One of our friends, Hmangchung, who had taken baptism in Lakhipur, sent a letter to me.

As soon as I received the telegram, I prepared to go to Haflong. I left Lakhipur on July 16, 1967, for Haflong. There I met a district council executive member and sub-divisional officer (SDO) who had been a classmate of mine in class six. I inquired, "Brother Vuana, we are from the same village. Not only the same village, but we are classmates. There was good friendship between you and me. This Pastor Lalhmudik is my pastor. Why do you do things like this?"

Mr. Vuana replied, "No, this is not my will. A pastor

came to my office and reported, 'Pastor Lalhmudik is an evil spirit. He spoke in other tongues. They have false doctrine, so if we don't stop him, he will spoil our Haflong City,' I had no time to prove it. I wrote a letter to the SP and the SP sent police to Brother Lalhmudik."

"Ah," I said. "This is your mistake. They may report anything, but you must prove it true or false. Before you proved the matter, why did you order this? Please write a letter for me to take to the magistrate, saying, 'This was a false report. Please release that pastor.'" I added that the UPC was recognized by the central government of India.

Mr. Vuana wrote a letter to the magistrate. "I received a false report from another pastor. That Pastor Lalhmudik is not an evil spirit."

I went to the magistrate. "Magistrate, today I want to bring back, to release, my pastor from your jail."

"Oh, I did not know anything. According to the report and according to the order from our executive officer, we did these things. If he writes an order like this, no harm. I will release him." That same day he released our pastor.

Pastor Lalhmudik worked very hard. He baptized several schoolteachers in Jesus' name. The district council tried to stop him but they couldn't. Now we have a big church in Haflong. I expect that someday they will become a separate district.

13 (1967-1974)
Shillong, Meghalaya

In 1967, the same year that our full gospel reached Tripura and North Cachar, I was invited to visit Shillong, now capital of Meghalaya State. A driver, Vaikhuma, had transferred from Silchar to Shillong. I went there for my first visit. God blessed me. Twelve people took baptism in Jesus' name.

When I visited Bhopal in southern India, I reported to Brother Harry Scism. When he heard these things he told me, "When you go back, we must visit Shillong. We shall see the conditions." Brother and Sister Scism, Damhuala, Muana, and I visited Shillong in March 1968 for meetings.

[Here Brother and Sister Harry Scism met Vaikhuma, the driver mentioned earlier, and heard his story. Sister Audrene Scism relates:

"When we were in Shillong, we rented a house and camped there. I fixed breakfast of bread, jam, and coffee. We couldn't cook there. Every day we walked four to five miles to market for food twice a day. One brother

Lera

who worked for the telephone company took us around and acquainted us with the town and with people who were interested.

"Brother Vaikhuma, the government driver, had an unusual experience. Several years previously, he'd been dragged out of his jeep by Mizo National Front rebels and lined up with others in front of a firing squad. When they tried to shoot him, the gun wouldn't fire. They tied him to a tree in the jungle and left him. He got loose and walked to his village. Meanwhile, he saw a tiger in the jungle on the way. By the time he got to his village, the rebels had found out he was loose. Some guards were stationed in front of his house to look out for him. He didn't know who they were, so he walked past them into his house. Either God closed their minds or their eyes, for they didn't recognize him. When he got inside, his wife and children told him the rebels were waiting for him and to run away. He went out the back door into the jungle and hid. During our meetings in Shillong, he received the Holy Spirit."]

When he saw the conditions, Brother Harry Scism decided, "Here in Shillong we need to have a headquarters. You need to move here. You need to start the work."

Right then he made the final decision to move my family to Shillong. "I will give you Rs 275 for travel allowance; then I will give you Rs 100 for your personal use. You must try to get the rest from the church."

I had six children and only Rs 275. If we looked at the money, we would not go happily. But I told him, "If I preach the gospel, God will provide for me. I'm not thinking about or depending on money. If you want to try it,

Shillong, Meghalaya

I have no objection."

On the way to Silchar we had a great accident. While we were going downhill, the bus brakes failed completely. The bus driver tried to go up a road on the right side. The back wheel stayed straight and our bus stopped while pointing uphill. Brother and Sister Harry Scism, who were also on the bus, say a tree stump caught against the rear axle.

We were not suffering, so we slowly got out. The Scisms later told me, "On that day, a certain lady had a strong burden to pray for Harry Scism. She wrote us, 'On that day I prayed so much for you. What was the matter?' "

The next day we reached Lakhimpur, where we had a district conference. Brother Scism announced, "Brother Lerthansung will move to Shillong, so we need to have an election for the district pastor." The people could not object since the superintendent said this. We elected Brother Tebonga as district pastor of Cachar.

My family moved to Shillong in May 1968. We rented a small house.

Before I visited Shillong, Brother Tebonga had baptized Brother Ngurchuaia in Jesus' name. However, he did not want to belong to the UPC, because in Shillong there were no UPC members. When I reached Shillong, I heard that he had taken baptism in Jesus' name. I then wrote a letter to him. "Brother Ngurchuaia, we must have a church committee meeting because you are the first UPC member in Shillong." At last he came to my house, and we had a discussion. "Now I'm going to start the work in Shillong. I'm a new person for Shillong. What shall we do?"

Lera

I wrote some gospel tracts that said: "I came to Shillong. I am a UPC pastor. Those who are feeling the Holy Spirit or who are thirsty for the Holy Spirit, please come. We shall pray for you." I distributed these tracts to the people.

The first Sunday we had a meeting, and a sister stood up. She was crying. "Oh, I have been watching and waiting for a spiritual pastor. I have some money to submit, but I do not want to submit it to the Presbyterian church, because they believe in the trinity. My tithe I want to give to a real pastor," she said. On that day she submitted Rs 300. Other people also gave. That first Sunday we received Rs 450.

Every first Sunday we took up a collection. It increased steadily, and our work also increased. Now by the help of God, we have in the city of Shillong two churches and two preaching points. This is now part of our UPC Central District.

The J. O. Wallaces conducted this Sunday school leaders seminar in Shillong during the 1975 general conference of Northeast India.

14 (1972-1974)
Establishing the Missions Department

When Brother Harry Scism came to Shillong, he said, "The UPC of Northeast India started in 1950. Now we have come to 1972. Twenty-two years. Now we need to have a missions department. We need to reach other countries. Every district has a district spirit. This is not good. We must work together, and we must send additional missionaries."

So we formed a missions department. Brother Scism appointed Brother Damhuala as general missions director and Brother K. L. Hnuna as general missions secretary-treasurer, because the one was our assistant superintendent and the other was our general secretary. However, since they had such a great amount of work in their jobs, they had no time to consider the missions work.

In 1974, when we had another missions conference, Brother Harry Scism requested Brother Damhuala's report about the missions work. Brother Damhuala said, "Oh, sometimes I forget that I am the director. Since I am working as assistant superintendent, I'm very busy. Though you appointed me as general missions director, I have no time to work at it. I have no report concerning the missions department."

[Being assistant superintendent involved much responsibility. As Brother Scism was at that time also superintendent for Sri Lanka and for Burma, as well as regional field supervisor for Asia/South Pacific, he delegated a great deal of his responsibility to Brother Damhuala]

Brother K. L. Hnuna was in the same condition—no report.

Brother Scism decided, "We need another missions director. Brother Lerthansung has always said for us to visit Andaman and other countries also, because he has a great missions vision. I will appoint him missions director." At this time I was district pastor in Shillong. "And Brother Ruata I will appoint as general missions secretary."

We took a collection for the missions fund and received Rs 474. In that conference we appointed Brother Vankhuma to move to South Tripura—the last unevangelized corner of Tripura—among the Riang people, the tribal people. "Brother Vankhuma, we appoint you as missionary to South Tripura. You will get Rs 300 per month. But as we now have Rs 474, you will have Rs 300 for your food and the balance for your travel fare."

Brother Vankhuma responded, "Yes, yes, I will go," and went to South Tripura.

Then we made an appeal to the districts. "Now we

Missions Department

have a missions department. Every district needs to give to the missions fund. We have already sent our national missionary to South Tripura. We promised to give him Rs 300 per month. Now we have only Rs 474 and I have already given that to him. What shall we do?" I stopped to visit every district and appealed to the people, "We need to preach the gospel to every creature."

By the help of God every district had a missions vision, and we were able to give regular help to Pastor Vankhuma. By the end of 1974 we had a balance of over five thousand rupees.

Trying on a suit E. L. Scism sent (1972).

Lera

Sister Sikhupi, ladies auxiliary president of Northeast India, presented this hand-woven cloth to Sister Vera Kinzie, president of the UPC ladies auxiliary. This cloth was sold to raise money for missions in Northeast India.

15 (1974)

Mikir Hills

On January 19, 1974, I went to preach in the Mikir Hills in Assam State. Earlier that month, Pastor Sehkholam had visited this place from Nagaland and baptized some members in the name of Jesus but soon left. Mikir Hills was in my district, so it was my responsibility to look after it. I went to Suangsang village to form a church.

The Mikir people are very tribal. They usually do not build their houses on top of hills, but prefer to build them in the valleys and live in villages under the thick forest. Each village consists of only five to ten houses. The men and women put on hardly any clothes except to tie some cloth around their waists. The women wear full necklaces and wear earrings.

Since they live in the jungle, they can hardly increase in number. They love hunting and mostly eat all kinds of animals, including snakes, rats, and monkeys.

I invited Brother Lalringa to come, and we went together. To reach Suangsang Village, we had to pass many elephants. On the way, we came to a place some farmers had cut trees and were burning jhum. We almost died when they set the fire. We ran as far as we could. That day I've never forgotten.

At last we reached the village. I started my ministry and presented the truth. All the people there were under the Presbyterian church. They were of mixed tribes. God placed them under the hearing of our full gospel, and thirty-six people were baptized in Jesus' name.

"If we become UPC, we need to separate from our old church," they told me. "During your stay, we need to try to finish our church building."

"Yes, yes," I responded. There was much sun grass and bamboo and many trees. We carried bamboo; we carried trees; we carried sungrass. We finished their church in a week.

Now the Mikir Hills is under our UPC Central District. By 1986 according to the report of Brother Ropara, the district pastor, we now have eight preaching points in the Mikir Hills. We have a good school there. Among the few Christians in Mikir we are in the majority.

The living conditions there are still very backward. When I went back to the Mikir Hills, a church elder wanted to invite me to take food with him, but he had no chicken or red meat. He decided to go to the jungle and make traps. God blessed him so much that the next day he caught twenty-six rats in his traps.

Then he invited me to lunch. Before eating, I prayed to God to purify the food. When we began to eat, the church elder said, "Oh, thank you, thank you, Brother Lerthansung. I wanted to invite you to take food with me, but we could not offer you chicken or other meat. But since we wanted to invite you for lunch in the name of Jesus, I went to the jungle and set a trap. I am sure God knew how much I wanted to invite you for lunch, for He blessed me with these rats that entered my trap. When I saw those jungle rats—the big ones—I was so happy. Do you like to eat them?"

"Yes, yes," I replied. "No harm. Any kind of food you can prepare I like very much. During my childhood, rat was my first meat." I know rats carry rabies and all kinds of diseases, but we don't care. He prepared it nicely. It was very, very tasty.

When our church elder cooked the rats I hadn't tasted them for many years. Later I told Brother Cook this story and he protested, "Oh, Brother Lerthansung, there is no need to eat another rat. You could be poisoned or get some disease."

"But by the help of God, before we eat, we pray to the Lord to sanctify everything," I reminded him.

During my childhood, we could not find any other meat except rats. At that time there were many rats in our house, and we killed them. Sometimes they crawled in under the house, and we took them from their homes. This was our first meat in our childhood.

We killed the rats by setting chilies on fire and sticking them in the rat holes. The smoke would kill the rats. They could not run out; they were trapped and killed. Then we could pull them out.

In our childhood we did not have any other meat except rats and dogs. Dogs are convenient for the hill people. When we invite some people to help us—perhaps thirty people to help repair our house—we kill two or three dogs. Then we prepare very good curry. These are not wild dogs; these are pet dogs who lie around our house.

Lera

We grab them suddenly. They are very, very useful for us. They help keep places clean by scavenging, and they are very convenient. So dogs and rats gave me my first experience in eating meat. Really, they're not so bad.

In 1984, when I first visited the Naga Hills with Brother Chunga, one of our friends found a jungle rat—a big one. We ate it in Kohima. They prepared it, but it smelled a bit too strong for me. However, Brother Chunga liked it very much.

[Chunga later said that he ate it because the Bible tells us, when we are given food while on the ministerial trail, to eat what is put in front of us without asking questions (Luke 10:7-8; I Corinthians 10:27; Mark 16:18). He was following the same precept that Lerthansung followed earlier—"Any kind of food you can prepare I like very much"—that is, gratefulness for hospitality offered. Chunga also points out that there are rats and then there are rats. Village rats eat all kinds of filth, but jungle rats and field mice feed on vegetation. This makes their meat better tasting and more healthful.]

The rat was very, very important for us. I was thankful to God that I could nicely eat the meat of rats. Our local church elder was also very happy that eating them was not difficult for me.

16 (1975-1984)
Nagaland

Dr. Sasekio wrote a letter to me in March 1959, telling me that my name was registered in the Indian Christian Handbook as Reverend Lerthansung, United Pentecostal Church, New Churachandpur, Manipur. His letter reported, "There is a great revival going on in Nagaland, especially in Kohima town. Many people are being baptized by the Holy Spirit, speaking in unknown tongues, and some have prophesied. Many miracles and healing services have happened, and we are very happy and overjoyed by these. But the leaders of the Baptist church cannot accept us; hence, we decided to separate from the Baptist church. Now we are greatly in need of leaders who can get along with us. I saw your name and that you belong to the Pentecostal church. I am sure you could accept the Holy Spirit that dwells among us." He told me to come to Kohima as soon as I had time.

From Churachandpur to Kohima is more than one hundred miles. I had a great desire to go there, but during those times there was great revival also occurring in

Lera

South Manipur and in many parts of Mizoram. I had no time to stay at home as I was constantly receiving calls from various places. Moreover, the Presbyterian church had persecuted and given false reports about those in Manipur and Mizoram who received the Holy Spirit. I was busy helping those people and traveling in various places. Also, in Mizoram the Presbyterian church could not accept the Revival movement and had captured and jailed more than four hundred persons who received the Spirit.

Before I could leave for Kohima, Dr. Sasekio and the Revival people called the Reverend Mr. Salvary, who belonged to the Ceylon Pentecostal Mission in Calcutta. When he reached Kohima, the members of the Kohima Revival movement joined the Ceylon Pentecostal Mission. I had to cancel my trip to Kohima. I still hope that God will bring these people to the Oneness message.

In 1975, since a great revival had broken out in the state of Nagaland, our executive board suggested that I go to Nagaland as a missionary to preach the full gospel to them. "Brother Lerthansung is already missions director. Better to request him to move to Nagaland."

According to the resolution of our executive board, I went to Nagaland. First I moved by myself. Before entering Kohima, the capital, I halted at Dimapur. That night I prayed, "Lord Jesus, I'm going to Nagaland, where I have never been before. I do not know even one person to welcome me. But I am going under Your guidance, so lead me in all my ways and show me how I should start my ministry. If You do not lead me, I cannot work in Nagaland." I concluded with a question. "What is important for Nagaland?"

Just after the completion of my prayer, God spoke

in my heart: Love the Naga people. If you do not love them, you cannot work.

I was very happy and decided, Tomorrow I am going to the booking office.

The next day, whomever I saw of the Naga people, I loved. I was full of love for the people and overjoyed. I realized that unless I had a love for them my ministry would be in vain.

At 10:00 AM I went to the Nagaland bus station. There were many people lying around in the booking office and many people in a queue for bus tickets. I was at the end. I thought, If I don't get a ticket, I will have to stay another day in Dimapur. At that moment a young man who was also in the queue for the same ticket saw me, came over, and asked who I was.

"I am Pastor Lerthansung."

"Where are you going?"

"I'm going to Nagaland."

"What will you do?"

"I will preach the full gospel in Nagaland as a missionary."

"Please give me your money. I will buy the ticket for you."

I gave him money, and he purchased tickets for both of us. We got in the front row—seats two and three. I was so happy.

[Indian bus rides, particularly when endured in the back seats, are unique and memorable experiences. In the company of an enthusiastic bus driver on a twisting, downhill, one-lane road, only the dead can enjoy life, and only those passengers leaning out the windows of the speeding vehicle can find relief, often to the disadvantage

Lera

of those in the rear seats also sitting beside open windows.]

We sat together and discussed many things all the way. We stopped two times. Then he told me, "Pastor, we are going to take a cup of tea." We had a cup of tea and some eggs also. I wanted to give him money, but the gentleman said, "No, no, no, you need not pay. I will pay, I will pay." Whatever expenses we incurred, he paid for himself and did not allow me to spend anything.

When we reached Kohima, he asked me, "Where are you putting up?" I didn't know. I finally remembered Brother H. L. Zaler, who worked in the post office, but I did not know where his residence was.

Then he told me, "There is a Mizo who works in the post office, the sub-post office. If you want to put up with him, I will help you." That was good, but I did not know the sub-post office address. However, that gentleman went to the post office. He asked for the sub-post office address and wrote it down. Then he called two coolies. On that journey, for my suitcase and bedding I required two coolies. There were no buses or rickshaws, so he ordered two coolies and paid what they were going to charge me. "This gentleman you must take up to the sub-post office master," he told them. Just before he departed he said to me, "Brother, now I am going to the southern side, and you are going to the northern side. If you stay in Kohima, I shall meet you again."

"OK, OK."

"Bye bye," he said, after giving me his name and address, and he left for his home town.

I went with the two coolies and put up at H. L. Zaler's house. After two months I tried to find that gentleman,

Nagaland

but nobody recognized his name. "We have never heard this name in Kohima," they said. Even after one year had passed, I could not find him. I was thinking that whenever I met him again I would present him with a necktie. After inquiring from many people, I found that nobody knew his name or address.

At last the thought came to me, It may be an angel of God sent to help me. It reminded me of the two people who were on the way to Emmaus when Jesus showed Himself to them. This I still think; this was the first wonder in Nagaland.

In May 1976 I started moving to Nagaland. I requested of Brother Ngullie Lotha, a Naga, "We need to visit the last corner of Nagaland, the place they call Konyak. During the British time they called it headhunter country. We must turn it into soul-hunter country."

But Brother Ngullie Lotha answered, "Brother, if we visit that area, you need to be careful. The people are fighting, village against village."

"Yes, yes. We are going to the Konyak area," I replied. We started to travel. From Kohima the trip took about three days. I reached the district headquarters, their capital which they call Mon.

While I roamed the district headquarters, I met the deputy commissioner. He invited me to take a cup of tea with him. While we had a cup of tea, he told me, "Pastor, since you are going to the Konyak area, you must remember that those people really hate it when others laugh at them. I will tell you this: all the people are naked. Though you may see many things to laugh at in their culture, you should not laugh in front of them, though their dress is very peculiar. If you see them, you will want to laugh, but if you laugh, they will kill you. So remember this."

"Yes, yes."

I took a taxi. I paid Rs 150 for only eight kilometers. The taxi drivers did not want to go to that area, because they had great fear. Therefore, the price was very high.

When I reached Chui Village, I saw some ladies gathering firewood. The ladies wore only a six-inch piece of cloth that hung on their thighs in front and back. Eagles and lions were painted nicely on their skin. Even their faces and breasts were painted and decorated. This was somehow a matter of competition among them.

I wanted to take a picture of the people carrying firewood in a basket, but they did not allow me. They spoke to me in Assamese, "No need, no need."

"No, I want to take your picture. I will give you money." I gave them one rupee each. Then they were so happy and agreed.

After I took their photo, they told their friends that a stranger would pay them one rupee each to take their picture. After twenty minutes, more than twenty people came around me saying, "Mister, give me one rupee. Then you can take my picture."

"No, no. I have insufficient money."

"If you have no money, give me cigarettes, cigarettes." All of them like cigarettes very much; even all the ladies smoke.

"I never smoke," I told them.

I went to the chief's house. His house was very long, about 180 feet long. It was very big.

On the left and right sides of the house the wall was full of animals' heads. In front, outside on the veranda wall, were skulls of their enemies. At the chief's house I counted 350 skulls.

The chief said, "Don't count just these. When we put up these skulls, sometimes the dogs take them out, so instead of the skull we put a stone in front of the house. Please count the stones, too."

"Oh, rajah, let me purchase one. I want to purchase a skull. Wherever I go, I want to take it and show our people."

"No, no, no, you cannot purchase one. Those who have the most skulls are great kings. This is a sign for our Naga kings. These show that I am a great king and a hero-king. You will understand why I will not sell and you cannot purchase."

I requested permission to snap the chief's photo, but he did not agree. He told me that many had taken his photo earlier, but it was a bad sign for them that he would not live long.

The people in this area have some unusual marriage customs. If a boy and girl want to be married, first the parents talk together. If they are in agreement, the boy comes to the girl's house. Her parents tell him, "We parents have already agreed to your marriage. Now you must take hold of our girl's hand and pull her toward your house. If you cannot pull her, then you cannot get married." Then he starts to pull the girl. But some young men are very weak, and some girls are very strong. If a young man cannot pull a girl to his house, then they cannot get married.

When I heard about this I thought, Oh, if I were living here, since I am so small, I would not be able to pull the girls, and I could not get married.

Lera

[There is some logic to the system. It requires a man to be able to control his wife, a necessity in a patriarchal society. But why would the girl struggle at all? If she wants to marry the boy, couldn't she just walk hand in hand with him to their new home? Lerthansung explains that she would lose face. By not resisting and by not playing hard to get, she would be saying that she is desperate, that nobody better than this boy wants her, that her alternatives are nonexistent. To show that she is desired by others, she has to put up a fight. In detail how different, yet in essence how similar this is to the Western way! Truly, the more things change, the more they stay the same. Of course, the Naga method has flaws, yet it produces marital stability at least as effectively as the West.]

In this area, the people never bury their dead in a grave. Two or three days after a death they put the body in a coffin and hang the coffin in a tree. After several months, when only bones are left, they take the bones out and keep them in the house. They put all the bones in a box so that the bones of their ancestors are mixed together. "This is the family box," they say.

[Since Nagaland is in the hills and can get very cold at night, if a guest stays overnight in this area at a house where no extra blankets are available, the host invites the guest to spend the night between two of his daughters. However, this is only for purposes of warmth. If the guest touches either girl with sexual intent, he asks for death.]

In 1976 Christianity had not yet spread among the naked people. Leaders of the Naga Revival people from Chui visited a village called Chinglong, and they reported the following story. When the Naga people received the Holy Ghost, they wanted to say, "Praise the Lord; hallelu-

Nagaland

jah!"

Their chief was very angry. "I don't believe your 'hallelujah.' I don't believe your 'praise the Lord.' My son died about four days ago and I hung him in the tree. Go to the tree. If you pray for my son and if he lives again, then I will believe your 'hallelujah.' Then I will believe your 'praise the Lord.'"

The revival leaders went to the jungle and prayed for boy. "Lord Jesus, we cannot tell them the gospel, but we need Your power. How can they become Christians? This we commit into your hand." They prayed very much. After their prayer, they shouted inside the coffin. Suddenly a sound came from it. The coffin was opened, and the boy stepped out from the coffin. He was about six years old. Then they led the boy back to his father.

When the headman saw his son alive, he was filled with happiness. The whole village accepted the Lord Jesus in September 1977. They received the Holy Spirit and spoke in other tongues.

At the same village a great revival broke out in 1978. Many people were baptized with the Holy Ghost. Another amazing story was reported by the Revival people in this area. At a meeting in February Brother Sanglong, seventeen years old, stood up and gave a message in tongues. A lady interpreted. "Listen, listen. Hear what he prophesied to you. Sanglong says, 'On the coming March 15, God will take me to heaven. Jesus is coming soon. You need not be troubled. I will not come back. Nobody should worry about me. When you see these things, you must remember that Jesus is coming soon."

On March 15, the village people gathered together in Brother Sanglong's house. Sanglong sat in the mid-

Lera

dle, holding a Bible. Just before they had prayer together, Brother Sanglong disappeared from his place. The people did not know what to do. It seemed like Elijah's disappearance.

They tried to find him during the months of March and April, but they could not find him. Then they reported the matter to the government of Nagaland. The government published the story in the newspaper *Uramail* on May 11: Brother Sanglong, about seventeen years old, of such-and-such a village in the Konyak area in Nagaland has been taken to heaven. If you see him come back, you need not be troubled.

Just before I left Nagaland, I met their pastor, Shehoto. He told me in March 1980, "To this point he has not come back. His father and mother are still looking for him and long very much for him. Sometimes they expect him to come back. Sometimes in the evening they look toward the sky. They expect him to come back, but according to prophecy he will not come back, because Jesus is coming soon.

"Due to the miracle at Chinglong Village, eight other villages were converted to Christianity. The revival leaders are saying that Sanglong will not come back, that it was a sign that Jesus' coming is very near."

Those eight villages are in the Konyak area. This area is still not peaceful. When there is a quarrel in the bazaar, the people fight village against village. All the men have two guns—single-barrelled and double-barrelled. They make them themselves, and the government cannot control them with gun licenses. Each man also has a big bow and a big spear. They are very smart.

According to the report of their magistrate, when

they kill a person, they do not want to use the body for curry, but for the sake of pride they cut some meat, fry it, and eat it. They like to boast, "I killed an enemy; I ate his flesh." As of 1986, according to the reports, the government is still working on criminal cases from 1974. Before Jesus comes they will not finish their criminal cases.

In Nagaland there are sixteen tribes. Each has its own language. Up to 1977 there had been no revival in the Sema area. The people there belonged to the Baptist mission. I distributed many gospel tracts written in their language to their pastors, but they still had no intention to receive the Spirit. Then a notable miracle was reported there, and subsequently the Sema area received the Holy Ghost.

One farmer in the Sema area went to his jhum. The people there build huts to make small jhum houses. Just before the farmer entered his jhum house, he saw a big owl sitting on top of the hut. He picked up a stone, but just before he threw the stone to kill the bird for food, something unusual happened. He later testified that the bird started talking fluently in the Sema language. "Brother, why do you want to kill me? You people of Sema have no desire to know about the Spirit, and now the coming of the Lord is very near. So go back to your home and tell the people that Jesus is coming soon and that in order for you to go to His kingdom and be saved, you must have the Holy Spirit. Go back, go back." The farmer began to shake all over. He was so afraid, he almost died.

Shivering, he proceeded toward his village. After several hours, he reached the village. Then he invited all the people to hear him. Just before he reported, his body

Lera

began to tremble very much. He was so afraid, like King Belshazzar: "Listen, listen, brothers and sisters, there is a big owl in my jhum." He told them that an owl had spoken in their Sema language, saying that they all needed to seek for the Spirit as the coming of Jesus is very near.

When he had finished, the people were filled with pain and started crying. They prayed together for God to fill them with His Spirit. That night revival broke out in the Sema area, and it is still going on.

When the people began to receive the Spirit the Baptist church would not accept them, so the Sema revivalists separated themselves from the Baptist church. I was invited to speak in the Sema Revival Church at Mokokchung. I told them that according to the Book of Ephesians we must have one Lord, one faith, and one baptism.

Another unusual miracle was reported by the Revival people in the Lotha area. The district headquarters is in Wakha. About six miles from there, in a place about half Christian and half non-Christian, some of the Christians received the Holy Spirit. One Sunday some members who had not received the Holy Spirit prayed, and others prayed for them. They exclaimed, "Praise the Lord, hallelujah!" and cried loudly. At that moment they felt their church lift up from the earth. Unlike most of our churches, which have only a packed dirt floor, that building had a wooden floor.

When the unbelievers saw this they thought, Oh, these Revival people are going up to heaven in their church. They came together and brought all their money. They submitted it through the window. "Lord, I want to go to heaven," they cried, and held onto the window.

Nagaland

After one and a half hours, the church settled back down. That Sunday, all the people became Christian. They prayed together and received the Holy Spirit.

The Lotha people now call that place their revival center. They erected a new church building, spending around Rs 160,000, or ($12,300). The people brought their own money for their church. When I met them, they reminded me of the Israelites, who received gold and other costly things from the Egyptians and used them for the Tabernacle. Like that the Naga people now have a beautiful church in that area. When I was in Nagaland, these things greatly impressed my heart. We need to go to the dark areas, but if we cannot reach them, we pray and believe that somehow God will work in miracles another way instead.

I greatly appreciate the Nagaland Revival people. When they receive the Holy Spirit, they like the holy life very much. They stop smoking and chewing *pahn* (betel nut) and drinking. They never touch anything intoxicating after receiving the new wine of the Holy Spirit. When I travel in Mizoram and other places, I tell our people that this is a good example for us.

Now, by the help of God, we have twelve churches in the UPC in Nagaland. I have great hope that it will go on.

Brother Tourngam was appointed as missionary to Nagaland, and my family and I moved back to Shillong in 1980. In addition to being missions director, I was appointed as vice principal of Calvary Bible Institute. I was very busy.

In April 1982 Brother Satinvela, superintendent of Northeast India, Brother Chunga, Brother Tourngam,

Lera

and I went to visit our headquarters in Nagaland. We planned to spend Good Friday at Zuphu, our mission field headquarters. We started from Kohima, and after driving more than eighty miles, we reached Jessemi. Jessemi was the site of a great battle between the British and the Japanese during the Second World War. After crossing this place, we neared the Burma border, where there was a big bridge guarded by the Border Security Force. It was a checkpoint where the guards checked all passengers. They checked the truck which carried us, bringing with them a small sheet of paper. On it were written the names Reverend Lerthansung, general missions director, and Reverend Satinvela, superintendent. They told us that anyone bearing these names must get out. We both got out and asked what was the matter.

The All-Naga Puturi Student Union had heard about us and wanted to kill us. They had threatened, "If you cross the Agas Bridge, you will surely die. You must not cross that bridge." There was the river Agas. There was the big bridge. The Border Security Force asked us, "Are you Reverend Satinvela? Are you Reverend Lerthansung?"

"Yes, yes."

"You cannot cross that bridge."

"Why?"

"This morning a number of students waited for you on this bridge saying that your purpose in coming to Puturi was to bring disunity among the churches. It was the order of the Puturi student leader to the Border Security Force to send you back. If we refused, they threatened to murder us."

We still tried to go, but the Border Security Force

warned us not to go, as trouble would arise not only for both of us but for them also. "The All-Naga Puturi Student Union is so angry because you disturbed the Baptist mission. When they heard your message, many people wanted to accept it. For that reason the Baptist mission leaders turned the students against you and the students want to kill you. So go back to Kohima."

While we were still talking, the students sent a message to the BSF leader, telling them not to send Reverend Lerthansung and Reverend K. Satinvela, as the students were waiting for them on Akhago Road. The BSF told us that it was best for us not to go, so we decided to go back to Kohima. We could not go forward, so we went back.

When we reached Kohima, six people were waiting for us. A police sub-inspector, Brother Thlamuana, and his friends had a great desire to take water baptism. "Today we want to take water baptism. When we heard you had come to Kohima, we came to Kohima from our village, but you had already left. We were praying and praying for you to come back."

That night seven people took water baptism in the name of Jesus in Kohima. Then the thought came to me, Our return from the Agas Bridge was really God's will. God wanted us to return to Kohima because there were some people who wanted to take water baptism in Jesus' name. This, too, is a miracle from God.

On April 4, 1984, at Mollen Village, where we had many members, our UPC building burned down at noontime. This happened while the members were in the fields. All their clothes, homes, and rice were burned also. Some are of the opinion that this was done by people who strong-

Lera

ly opposed the UPC.

In order to help these victims, the Shillong headquarters and our UPC members started collecting clothes and other donations. To distribute our collection, I went to Kohima along with Brother P. Chunga. This time God opened our way, for Brother Khawsiama, deputy superintendent of police, had come with us. We all went in his police jeep to Mollen. We then called all the mission field workers to Zuphu and distributed the clothes and the money we had collected.

During this time, some student unions tried to make trouble for us and sent a police sub-inspector and some student leaders. But when they learned that DSP Joseph Khawsiama was along with us, they were very afraid and told us a lie, saying they had come for other reasons. Brother Joseph Khawsiama then told the police that unless it were the order of the government, they had no right to interfere in religious matters. He told the police not to interfere with the UPC or with any religious concern. It appears that God guided our way through the help of Brother Khawsiama. So now the UPC has been established in Nagaland, and is still reaching more villages.

"This is the headhunting area of Nagaland. We shall turn it into a soul-hunting area now. Who wants to pray for me?"

17 (1979)

Andaman Islands

The Andaman Islands are more than twelve hundred miles from Calcutta in the middle of the Bay of Bengal, and they consist of about three hundred small islands. In the days of the British, there was a great penal colony where convicts were imprisoned for life. There are two kinds of naked people who live in the thick forest. One tribe is called Onge, and the other is called Jarwa. These naked people do not speak like us. They have bows and arrows for shooting animals and men. The people who live in the villages are very backward both naturally and spiritually.

In 1972 I felt God calling me to go there, but I did not have an opportunity as the place is not easy to visit. But, thank God, Brother Satinvela and I went to the Andaman Islands on April 29, 1979. We flew from Calcutta and after one hour and fifty-five minutes we landed at the Port Blair airfield. There we met Pastor Fouj Singh and went to Cuddle Gunj village about twenty-one miles from Port Blair, the capital of Andaman.

Lera

Pastor Fouj Singh had belonged to the Ceylon Pentecostal Church. I met him in Cachar, and after hearing the truth, he received water baptism in the name of Jesus.

Brother Satinvela and I stayed about nine days in the Andaman Islands. After hearing our message, twenty people took water baptism in the name of Jesus. Now we have three preaching points in Andaman Islands under the guidance of Pastor Fouj Singh.

Pastor Fouj Singh and Lerthansung in Andaman.

18 (1979-1983)
Bangladesh

After returning to Shillong from Nagaland, I received a letter from the country of Bangladesh. Brother Satinvela and I made application for a visa to go there. Although Bangladesh is a neighboring country to India, it is very difficult to visit. It was not possible for Brother Satinvela and me to get a visa at that time. Yet we could not forget the people of Bangladesh because they wanted to hear our full gospel.

We again applied for visas. By the help of God we got them this time. However, Brother Satinvela was suffering from jaundice. The doctor requested him to take rest since his health was not good, so I had to go alone.

On July 8, 1979, I reached Calcutta and stayed in the Hotel Embassy. Then I started praying, "God, I know not anyone in Bangladesh, and I have never been there, so I put everything in Your hands for You to guide my way and help me in my ministry. Let it be according to Your plan."

The next day I left for Calcutta airport. A certain

Lera

gentleman stood in front of me at the airport counter. When we produced our tickets, we had to pay a travel tax of about fifty rupees. He had no money in Indian rupees, and he had no time to get his money changed, so he was very troubled. When I saw his trouble, I told him, "Brother, don't worry. I will help you. I have one hundred rupees—enough for you and for me." He was very happy. We both cleared everything in the Calcutta airport.

When we were finished with customs and other formalities, we met together outside and took a cup of tea before we entered into the airplane. The gentleman asked me, "Brother, who are you? You loved me so much that through your kindness I was able to go through easily. I'm very happy, so may I know your name?"

"Yes, yes. My name is Lerthansung. I work as the general missions director for the United Pentecostal Church in Northeast India. I came from Shillong. Now I am going to preach the gospel in Bangladesh."

"I'm so glad to meet you. I am Dr. Paroi. I work in Khulna Christian Hospital. I am in charge; I am a medical officer. Bangladesh Christians selected me to attend the conference of the World Council of Churches. I went to Switzerland, and now I've come back. I had no time to go out anywhere, so I had no Indian money. For that reason I was troubled. Brother, you need not be troubled, though. When we land in Dacca, I will help you however I can."

When we landed in Dacca I knew nothing about Bangladesh. He took my passport and documents. "Please follow me. I will go first." I followed him.

Many customs officers and other people knew him

Bangladesh

very well because he was a big medical officer. They began to greet him. "Oh, Dr. Paroi, you've come back, you've come back. Praise the Lord." Then they added, "Did you bring anything?"

"Oh, if you want to, you can open my suitcase. I put in some underpants and towels."

They did not want to check it but asked, "And who is this?"

"This is my good friend. We came together from India."

"Shall we check his suitcase?"

"If you want to check, no harm. I think he may have some shirts and underpants. If you want to check, go ahead."

Then the customs officers replied, "No need to check it." So without being checked we got out.

Dr. Paroi asked me, "Brother, where are you going to stay?"

"I've never visited here. I am a new person to Bangladesh. Some people advised me to go to the Purnama Hotel."

"No, no, no, the Purnama Hotel is a big hotel. Very, very high. Only some foreigners and some high officers can stay there. You must go to the YMCA guest house. I will lead you."

When they saw the doctor at the guest house all the people there stood up. "Oh, Dr. Paroi, you came back, you came back!" Then they saluted him.

He talked to the manager. "This is my good friend. We came together from India. Please...the best room for him. He has no time to change his money. While he is in Dacca, as much as he needs, you advance to him.

Lera

You must trust him; this is a good man."

We went back to the air office, for the doctor said, "Brother, from the foreigners the people who are working in the air office try to receive extra money. So we must go together."

When they saw him, they stood. "How are you, doctor? You've come back. Yes, yes. What do you want?"

"This is my friend. He needs to go back to Calcutta on such and such a date. We need to confirm his ticket."

"Please give it to me, please give it to me," they said. Suddenly they did it and finished it. We came back and took food together.

Then the doctor told me, "Brother, I want to sleep tonight, but I already informed all my district of my arrival. They'll come to the city and they will welcome me, so I cannot cancel my program. I will leave you." Just before he left me, he rang up the Bangladesh Christian Union central secretary, the Reverend Adikari. "Brother Adikari I brought a good pastor from Shillong. I cannot help him, for now I must leave for my district. Please help him."

"Yes, yes. Don't worry. I will come."

Then Dr. Paroi left. Just after he left, the secretary came in his car. "Are you Reverend Lerthansung?"

"Yes, yes."

"Please come to my office." We went there and talked together. After a cup of tea, he informed the missionaries and pastors in Bangladesh, "Reverend Lerthansung has come from Shillong. He is going to preach the full gospel in Bangladesh. Those who want to meet him can meet him freely. He is staying in the YMCA, room number such and such."

Bangladesh

I stayed about four days. During my stay in Dacca, I met many missionaries and pastors. I taught about the one true God, baptism in Jesus' name, and speaking in tongues. I distributed tracts to all the pastors. I requested that I be allowed to attend their church, but the pastors explained, "We cannot have regular church meetings. Only on Sunday can we even have Sunday school for our children. We are so sorry about this." Since none of the churches could have regular church meetings, they were almost abolished.

I took advantage of the situation to make my point. "Brother, this is good. If we do not stand in the Bible truth, in the apostles' truth, though we have a big building and a big degree, we have nothing."

After four days I flew to Chittagong. When I landed at the Chittagong airport so many people had friends, but I was alone. I entered the airport bus. The driver said, "Where are you putting up?"

"Oh, I don't know. Take me to the city office. Then I will consider where to stay."

He laughed and laughed. "Since you are a foreigner, before you landed, you should have reserved a hotel room."

"No, I didn't know where there were hotels. Where am I putting up? I don't know. I am new here. I've never visited before."

When I reached the city office I asked a gentleman, "I have come from Shillong. I am a foreigner to Bangladesh. Where shall I put up?"

"There is the Embassy Hotel. You can put up there." It was not far, so I walked.

When I entered the Embassy Hotel, the manager

Lera

said, "If you have no Bangladesh taka [their currency], we cannot admit you."

"I have some Bangladesh taka. If you cannot take American dollar checks, I have some Bangladesh taka." When I gave some, they admitted me.

That night I prayed and prayed to God. "Lord, I am a new person to Bangladesh. Whom should I contact? Whom should I meet? How can I preach your gospel?"

In the early morning, I went up near the top of my hotel and looked around. I saw a big building with a sign and a cross. "That house is a type of church, I thought. There will be a pastor. I will go." Before breakfast I went.

When I knocked on the door I met a *chowkidar* (watchman). He asked me, "Who are you?"

"I am a pastor from Shillong. Do you have a pastor here?"

"No, we have no pastor, but we have missionaries from England."

"Please show me to their place."

When I knocked, the missionary opened his door. "Who are you?"

"I am Pastor Lerthansung from Shillong."

"You came from Shillong?"

"Yes, yes." Then he went back in his room and called his wife. Fortunately, they had one child—a boy. When the baby was ready to be delivered, they had come to Shillong's Robert Hospital. So when I mentioned Shillong, they were very happy.

The man told his wife, "This brother has come from Shillong." "We just came from Shillong," they said at the same time. "Please come in, please come in. We are going to have breakfast. Do you want to join us?"

"Yes, yes." It was a very simple breakfast. They had a big loaf of bread, one banana, some jam, and a cup of tea.

While we were eating breakfast, I talked to them frankly. The man, whose name was Olben, was very young. "I have come to Bangladesh, and I want to invite some Christian leaders who are working among the Chittagong Hill Tract people. I have some friends from when I was in Bible college. However, if they come to Chittagong, we'll have no place to meet. Can we rent your church?"

"No, we have a big church building, but we have no members. We have no regular church services, so the YMCA rented my house and our church for a bookstore." That was why their house was full of books.

"Then please tell me whom I should contact." He wrote down all the pastors' names, churches, and addresses.

After breakfast, I went to the Assemblies of God church. Their secretary's name was Yung; he was from China. We talked together. "Mr. Yung, when do you have church meetings? I also want to attend."

"No, no, no, sir," he told me. "We do not have regular church. We're very strict. Smokers and those who chew pahn [betel nut] we cannot accept as members. For this reason, all the Bengali people flew from our church. So we do not have church meetings. It's completely empty. Since you have come, don't worry. I want to invite you to dinner."

"Yes, yes, I will accept," I answered. He was a young man and he operated a Chinese hotel.

After lunch I went to the Sweden Pentecostal Church, where I met Reverend Holder, a Bengali. When I entered

Lera

his home, I first met his wife. They had some gospel tracts. His wife told me, "My husband is suffering from jaundice, so he cannot move. If you want to meet him, come." Then she led me to their bedroom, and I talked to him.

The Reverend Holder said, "Oh, pastor, I am so happy that I could meet you. The Sweden Pentecostal Church wrote that they could not continue their church work. They withdrew from Bangladesh. I am alone, but I do not want to join another church. I tried to find a good Pentecostal organization, but I did not know whom I should join. God sent you this time. I am very happy. Please consent to have me as a pastor."

Then I told him frankly, "Brother Holder, you are already a pastor under the Sweden Pentecostal Church, but in the United Pentecostal Church after you take baptism in Jesus' name you need to preach about six months. Then if you are qualified, we can give you a license. Only then can we appoint workers. Now we are going to have a Bible seminar. It will be good for you."

"Yes, yes," he said.

After that, I left him and went to the Baptist Church. The pastor's quarters were in a nearby house. I met the Reverend Chaudhāry. He greeted me and asked, "Who are you?"

"I am Pastor Lerthansung from Shillong. I want to preach the gospel, so when do you have a church meeting?"

"Oh, I am very ashamed. We do not have a church meeting. Our building is very big, but we have no members. What to do? I want to resign my pastorate, too. I want to find another good organization. I was born near Gauhati. I want to go back to India. I do not want to stay in Bangladesh."

We had a cup of tea in his house. "Pastor, if possible, we want to rent your house for a Bible seminar."

"Yes, yes. No need to rent it. You can occupy it for the time being. For me it's a very shameful thing because we can't have meetings."

After I left there, I went to the Evangelical Presbyterian Church. A man opened the door and exclaimed, "Oh, you're Lerthansung!"

"Yes, yes."

"Oh, I thought the rapture had taken place." He was a classmate when I attended the trinitarian Bible college in 1949. Since 1949 we had never gotten together—almost forty years ago.

I answered, "No no, I am still the same Lerthansung."

"Then come in, come in."

He was having a pastoral committee meeting. At that moment nine pastors were sitting there together. He introduced me to his friends. "This is Brother Lerthansung. When we were in Bible college, he was our monitor, and I love him very much. He's a good preacher. All our principals also loved him very much, and I always talk about him."

All the pastors agreed, "Yes, this is the man you always talk about."

While they continued their meeting, I took a bath. Afterward, their secretary said to me, "Oh, pastor, we are very sorry. We have a problem. We are going back from Chittagong to the Chittagong Hill Tracts. This evening we need to go. What shall we do? When we come back, you'll have no more time, since your days are very limited."

"Yes, yes, but before you leave us, we must do some talking, so I want to invite you to take food at the China Hotel." This was the best hotel in Chittagong—very costly. I told Brother Dolian, my friend, "I have not much experience here, so select from this menu as you like. Don't worry about money. By the help of God, I will pay." While we were eating together, they were very happy. They had never eaten in this hotel because they were in a very poor economic condition.

I told them, "We want to start a work here. In the United Pentecostal Church, we have a great burden for Bangladesh. We want to present the full gospel. We don't care about your organization, but we want to present the full gospel. What shall we do? If you arrange a Bible seminar, we shall set the time. We shall pay the fare of the people who come to Chittagong and help them with food and lodging." They were very happy.

At that time, they represented three organizations. We planned six programs through their advice. Then *I* was very happy.

After we made our plans, all the pastors left Chittagong. As they left, the Presbyterian church secretary arrived back in Chittagong to prepare by-laws and manuals. He wanted to preach in English. The departing pastors said, "Oh, how very convenient. Our secretary, Brother Sumlal, has arrived in Chittagong. You can stay together and he will help you. Don't worry."

So I invited Brother Sumlal to stay with me in the Embassy Hotel. "Brother Sumlal, don't worry. Please come. You must stay with me."

"No, no, this is very expensive for me. This is impossible."

"But this time, by the help of God, we must work together and we must talk together. All the bill I will pay." Then he was very happy. We sat and ate together. He had never eaten such food before. His stomach and his heart were very happy. At that time I presented our gospel message.

I stayed in Chittagong three days. On the fourth day, he saw me off and gave me his address also. "When you come back, I will send some workers to attend your Bible seminar."

When I flew back to Calcutta, I reported to Brother Harry Scism. He was very happy that we could have a Bible seminar program. This was our first program for Bangladesh.

According to our plan, Brother Satinvela and I visited Bangladesh to have Bible seminars. After six visits and three Bible seminars, the people who attended were convinced of the truth. At first we did not want to pressure them too much; we wanted to convince them of the truth. After three Bible seminars, all the people were completely convinced. They completely changed their minds. That was in 1983 in Rangamati.

Then we started baptismal services. That time, four pastors, one evangelist, nine church elders and two nurses took water baptism in Jesus' name. On the day we were baptizing I invited a Roman Catholic priest who had come from France. We invited him to take food with us. He was lonely since there were no other foreigners in that place. When we met together, he was very happy. Even though we were not from Europe, he was still very happy.

I told him, "Please come to the water. The people are

Lera

going to take water baptism in Jesus' name. This will be a new experience for you."

"Yes, yes, I will come."

When I entered the water, Pastor Laithang of the Chittagong Hill tribes came first. He was very, very tall; I could not touch his head. I asked him, "Brother, please come down." I thought, If we were fighting physically, he could kill me easily because he's a tall, big, strong man. But for the sake of God, by the power of the true gospel, he keeps quiet while he waits for what I say: "Please stand, please sit, please bend down."

Brother Laithang was a new person to Christianity. In 1976 the Mizo National Front went to the Chittagong Hill Tracts. At that time, he was an unbeliever. Brother Laithang explained to me, "The MNF told us, 'If you are not a Christian, we will kill you.' We did not know what was necessary to become a Christian, but the MNF forced us. We did not want to be killed, so we gave them our names and became Christians. The MNF said, 'In the future you will know what is necessary and what the benefits are. You will understand.' Now that is true. By force I became a professing Christian. Now I know the truth. I have received the Holy Spirit."

"Pastor Laithang, according to your faith and according to your confession, I baptize you in the name of Jesus for remission of your sins." Then I baptized him. Fifteen people took baptism in Jesus' name. Then we came back to the house and prepared food.

There the Roman Catholic father talked to me. "Pastor Lera, when you baptize people, you never say 'Father, Son and Holy Spirit.' You say only 'Jesus.' This is too short for me."

"Oh, sir, the apostles never repeated 'Father, Son, and Holy Ghost.' Look in Acts 2:38. Peter told them, 'Repent, and be baptized every one of you in the name of Jesus Christ.' He never repeated 'Father, Son, and Holy Ghost.'"

Then he opened his Bible. "Hey! Thousands of times I've read this book, but I've never read this portion." We talked together about the trinity and about the one true God also. He confessed, "I've never heard this teaching. I think if we compare your teaching with the Bible it is true." If we could have stayed one more day, I think he would have accepted the truth.

We appointed a secretary and district pastor and some evangelists. We organized and established the UPC in Bangladesh. Praise the Lord!

Their most important need was a small boat. That area is full of water, so we purchased a beautiful boat for fifteen hundred taka (less than fifty-four dollars). We gave them money for their headquarters church also, since in Chittagong we had no headquarters and their headquarters was a bit far.

As for regular help we said, "We have no authority since you are foreigners to us. We will appeal to the international headquarters and see what they can do." We appealed to the headquarters, and they agreed to send one hundred dollars every month from that time.

One hundred dollars is quite a bit for them. It is over two thousand Bangladesh taka. Before the pastors came to the UPC, they got three hundred Bangladesh taka (about $11.50) per month. But we arranged that the district pastor should get six hundred taka and the others over five hundred taka. They were very happy.

Lera

After we established the church, the other denominations were not so happy. They reported to the government, "Reverend Satinvela and Reverend Lerthansung, when they came to Bangladesh, spoiled our church. They made trouble among us." For that reason, in 1985 we completely failed to get visas. In 1986 also we made application to the visa office, but I do not have much hope. We shall see.

I told our general secretary-treasurer, Sister Biaka, "If you can go to Dacca, try to meet the home ministry. Go there and report to us, for we do not have much hope of coming again."

"Yes, I will do as much as I can," she answered.

When Brother George Shalm visited, he requested that the church make by-laws and register with the Bangladesh government. After they registered, they opened an American Express bank account in the name of the UPC. Now they can receive funds directly from America to Bangladesh.

The people's condition is very poor in Bangadesh. They do not have good cultivation. Also, the people in the hill area have been neglected.

One remote tribe in the Chittagong Hill Tracts and in Burma is the Miri. The people do not generally wear clothes, only a small piece of cloth. Their customs are very different. Traditionally, when a woman was going to deliver a child, they took her out into the street and called everyone to watch the child's delivery. The midwife who delivered the child was given the placenta for curry. But now that they have become Christians, they do not carry on these old customs.

The revival movement began and continues among

our UPC. It's increasing steadily. Now there are more than four hundred baptized members in Bangladesh. We have sections and have appointed sectional presbyters, including Brother Laithang.

If we could go there one more time, we want to teach about pastoral duty and leadership training. We already finished some Bible courses about the one true God, baptism in Jesus' name, and the baptism in the Holy Spirit. But they need to learn about leadership.

God will arrange it somehow. Six times we had no trouble with visas, but after we disturbed some other churches, they reported us to the government. Still, we have established the church, and God will help them somehow. If we cannot contact them, but they stand firmly, then our missionaries and our regional supervisor can contact them. They can carry on the work.

Since we could not continue to travel to Bangladesh, we tried to reach another area that we had never visited. We contacted Sikkim.

At Kaptai Lake at Rangamati in 1983, our second baptismal service in Bangladesh. About fifteen people took water baptism in Jesus' name.

Lera

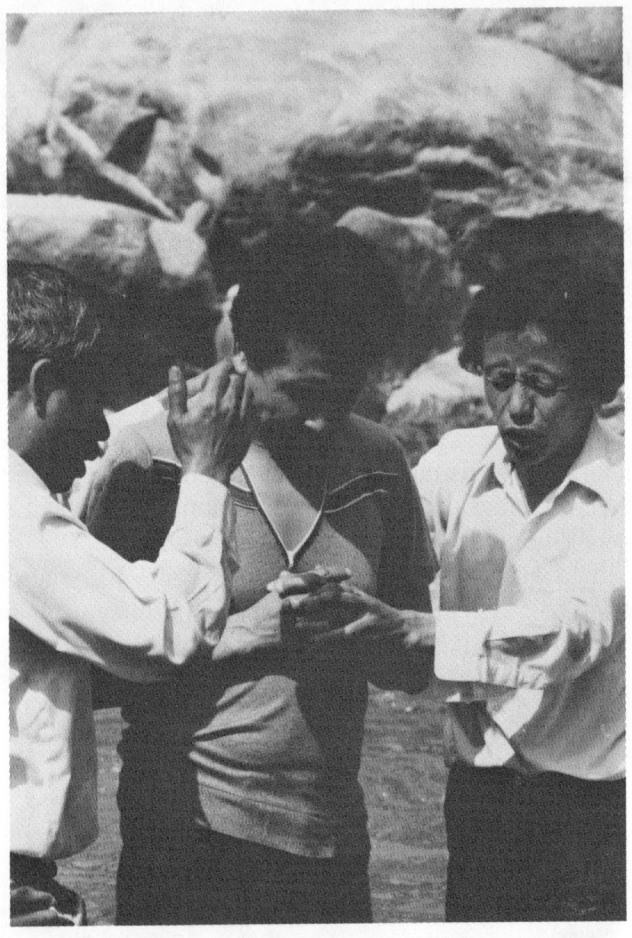

Pastor Marshal Gurung baptizing a trinitarian pastor in Jesus name.

19 (1983)

Sikkim

Sikkim was formerly an independent country on the border of Tibet. It was absorbed into India in 1974. I had the opportunity to baptize two trinitarian Pentecostal pastors in Sikkim—Brother G. B. Rai in Gangtok, the capital, and Brother Paul in Pangkhyong.

When we contacted Sikkim, Brother Satinvela and I visited first. When we had our first meeting, Brother Satinvela, since he was the superintendent, was asked, "Please start this—give a sermon." This was in Gangtok in Brother Joseph Tamang's house.

Brother Satinvela gave the message, but before he gave the message, he said that though they did not belong to the UPC, they were going to become UPC.

After the sermon, Dr. Gollay, their secretary, stood up. "Reverend K. Satinvela, we did not invite you because we are going to join the UPC. We invited you to hear your message. We are not concerned about your organization. Since we heard you are a full gospel preacher, we want to hear the full gospel." They had a great misunderstanding.

We went back to Shillong. They wrote a strong letter to us. "Reverend K. Satinvela and Reverend Lerthansung, you need not come back to Gangtok. You need not send any letters to Gangtok."

I wrote a letter secretly to Pastor G. B. Rai and Joseph Tamang through Brother Lawmkima, one of our Mizo people who was working in Sikkim. "Brother Lawmkima, please call them to your house and give them this letter. If other people know, they will not be happy."

My letter to them stated, "Brother Joseph Tamang and Brother G. B. Rai, we received your strong letter, but this I understand is not your real mind. When we presented you the truth, you accepted it from the bottom of your heart. Since you had already accepted the truth in your heart, this letter I can understand has been influenced by Satan. If you want to accept this truth, we shall appoint you as pastor. Then we will come down to Siliguri. You will have a post at Siliguri, from which you will look after Sikkim."

At first, they did not reply, but they tried to convince their people of the truth. I sent another letter and some tracts. After four months, they had convinced all the people. They accepted the one true God. They wanted to accept baptism in Jesus' name.

When they realized that the people had accepted the truth, they took a vote. "Now we are going to take a vote in our church. Those who want to take water baptism in Jesus' name, please raise your hand." Only two people did not raise their hands—the doctor and his friend. All the other people wanted to take water baptism. "If this is so, we are going to join the UPC," they announced.

So Dr. Gollay and his friend went out from the church.

Since all the people wanted to join the UPC, they made a resolution and then wrote a letter to me. "Brother Lerthansung, please come. We have already accepted the truth, and we want to take water baptism in Jesus' name." I was very happy. When I arrived, all the people were very happy.

From Gangtok down to the Ranipur River is more than five kilometers. The jeep driver charged Rs 120. Because of regulations of the government, which is very strict, the driver did not want to take more than seven people. We had many people. I told them, "We need not worry about the money. First, I am going in the jeep with six people. I will baptize them. Then they will go back. Then another seven people will come. I will wait for you in the water."

Six times they came and went back like that.

I was alone in the water until the next group arrived. Sometimes I bathed while waiting. I thought that John the Baptist must have been like me.

At that time, thirty-six people took water baptism. After that, the matter of first importance was to be registered with the government. This I told Brothers Joseph Tamang and G. B. Rai. They made application to the registrar's office, but the other churches had a central committee that tried to influence the registration of societies. Their joint committee passed and submitted a resolution asking the government not to register the UPC.

They tried to meet the chief minister, but Brother G. B. Rai knew the chief minister very well and told him, "Every organization can register according to the government rules. We are registered with the central government and in Shillong for the Northeastern Zone. Why can't you register us?" Then the chief minister recommended us, so we registered quickly.

When Dr. Gollay realized we were already registered, he wanted to come back, I was told. However, I had no time to go back to meet him. If I cannot ever go back to Sikkim, I hope Dr. Gollay will still come back. He has a Ph.D. and is a highly educated person.

This is the work of Sikkim.

The church in Gangtok, Sikkim.

20 (1983-1986)
West Bengal

Brother G. B. Rai contacted a friend who worked in the nearby district of Darjeeling, West Bengal State, in a place called Tukvor. This was Brother Marshal Gurung. They had gone to Bible college together in Dehra Dun. Brother G. B. Rai convinced that pastor of the truth, and they invited me to visit there. I told our superintendent, "Brother Satinvela, it would be good for us to go together to Tukvor."

"Yes, yes," he said. He was happy to come with me.

On November 24, 1984, he and I went to Darjeeling, to Tukvor Tea Estate, where there was a congregation of about eighty-five members in a trinitarian Pentecostal church.

We found a good relationship with the Tukvor church. After we talked about the one true God and about our full gospel and the name of Jesus, suddenly the Holy Spirit began moving among them. They started crying and dancing and cried out, "Jesus is the name of our God." They wanted to take water baptism in the name of Jesus, but the river was too far and there was no vehicle. Pastor Marshal Gurung said, "There is no convenient water for baptism. Though I am pastor for this church, first I will take water baptism, then I shall turn the people toward this truth."

Having no time for a baptismal service, we came back from Darjeeling to Siliguri on the way to Calcutta. We went to the river and baptized Brother Marshal Gurung. Then he went back and convinced his people.

After that he wrote a letter to me. "Please come. Some people want to take water baptism." We made plans that in March 1985 all the congregation would take water baptism in the name of Jesus. I invited Brother Hnezova to accompany me.

From Tukvor the river is about fifteen miles. We hired a small three-ton truck for Rs 150. As many people as we could we put inside the truck. About twenty-seven people took water baptism in Jesus' name.

There was a small plot of land that the owner wanted to sell. The Full Gospel Church wanted to purchase that plot for twenty thousand rupees and so did the Assemblies of God, but the owner told them, "This land I promised to sell to the UPC for ten thousand. If I sell it for twenty thousand, it is not so good. I will wait until April. If they do not buy it, then I will contact you and sell it to you."

If we did not purchase the land, there would be no place for the church building. I invited Brother Marshal Gurung to come to the district conference in Lunglei, Mizoram. There I appealed to the executive board to make a donation of ten thousand rupees.

On Saturday night they gave me a chance. I stood in front of the people. "Brothers and sisters, we have a big church in Lunglei. We are dancing. We are very happy. But our people have no church building. There is a convenient place. If we do not purchase it, then there is no other place at all. They requested ten thousand, but other church people want to give twenty thousand. The owner is waiting for us until April, so by the help of God we must purchase this. First I want to appeal to the superintendent. I will see how much he will give."

He pledged, "I will give two hundred."

Next I appealed to the secretary. He promised over two hundred rupees.

Then I appealed to the executive board, to all the departments, and to the district headquarters of each district. This was equivalent to appealing to all the pastors, since all our local church money goes into the district fund, from which pastors and evangelists are paid. After this appeal, we took up a collection from the people. By the help of God, we collected Rs 10,100 that night. The addition Rs 100 paid for registration fees.

When Marshal Gurung went back, he purchased the land. I had told him, "Brother Gurung, before you purchase, since this is under the tea garden area you must get permission from the tea garden manager. And you are under the control of the Communist Party." (It controls the state legislature in West Bengal.) He got no objection from the political party or from the tea manager, so we purchased that land.

In 1986 the people appealed to me to build a church building. But this time I did not want to appeal to the general conference. "First, as far as you can, try to collect for yourself. Then try to build a small hut or temporary building. We shall ask some of our friends and we

Lera

shall report to headquarters also. The time will come when God will supply this need."

This is the work of God in the Darjeeling church.

The story of Brother Christopher in Siliguri, West Bengal, is like that of Philip and the eunuch. While I was in Nagaland, I went to our conference in Aizawl. My family and I went to the train, but we couldn't get reserved seats, so all my family I pushed through the windows. Entering through the door would have been impossible, so I pushed them through the window. Then at last I entered.

A gentleman seated there saw me. "Brother, if you want to sit here, come sit with me."

"No, no, I will not sit. I will give the seat to my wife." After she sat down, the man and I talked together. "Who are you?" I asked.

"I am Pastor Christopher from West Bengal. I am trying to find a good organization, a Pentecostal group. I am going to Aizawl to find a good organization."

"If you want a good organization, I will tell you frankly—we have the best organization in the world. I cannot say we have good church buildings or good food or good support. But in the United Pentecostal Church we stand on the apostles' truth."

On the way to Aizawl we talked together about our doctrine. He tried to find another good organization in Mizoram, but he could not find one, so he came back and we met together in Shillong. "Brother, I tried to find a good organization in Mizoram. They have good church buildings, but their condition I don't like." When we talked together in Shillong, he completely changed his mind and wanted to join us. "When I go back to my home,

West Bengal

I will contact all our people. Then I will write to you."

After he went home and contacted all his church, all the people wanted to take water baptism. Then he wrote a letter to me. When I received his letter, I invited Brother Satinvela. "Since you are the superintendent, you need to come with me. Now we need to open a new field, and I do not want to go alone." Brother Satinvela was very happy. We went together.

When we reached Siliguri, we did not know the exact place to go. If we had known the place, we would have only needed to give Rs 5. Since we did not know the exact place, we hired a taxi and paid Rs 250. We tried and tried to find the address, and at last we did.

When we reached the place, Brother Christopher had a meeting. The people wanted to take water baptism the next day, but I did not want to baptize them. I told Brother Christopher, "Before you take water baptism, I want to explain what is so important about water baptism. After you hear what is so important, it will be a benefit to you. I will teach two or three times concerning baptism and concerning the trinity versus Oneness." After my teaching we went to the river.

The river was a little far from that place so we hired a bus. The people who were to take water baptism numbered twenty-seven.

First I went into the water and prayed. After I prayed, then Brother Christopher came into the water and I baptized him in Jesus' name. Afterwards he did not want to come out but began swimming. I told him, "Brother Christopher, this is not the time to bathe."

"No, very warm, very warm. I want to swim," he replied. He swam, so all the people did not want to leave after taking water baptism. They began swimming and taking baths. In Mizoram and the Northeast, after we baptize people, they come out of the water and we pray for them to receive the Holy Ghost. But with these people this was not possible since after taking water baptism they were so happy that they wanted to take baths and swim.

Brother Satinvela finally said, "Oh, no harm. If they do not want to pray here, we will pray in the church." That night we prayed for them to receive the Holy Spirit and some of them did. We appointed a church secretary, a church treasurer, and a church committee. Then we came back to Shillong.

After one month I received a letter from Brother Christopher. "Brother Lerthansung, please come to West Bengal. We have some candidates for baptism." I went back.

At one place on the border between the countries of Bhutan and India, there is a gatekeeper named Lalbahadur. He was baptized in Jesus' name. After three days he invited me to take food with him. He prepared goat meat. Just before we ate he gave his testimony.

"Brother Lerthansung, I want to give a testimony. Some years back, I wanted to become a Christian, but my father was an orthodox Hindu so he refused to allow me. 'If you want to become a Christian, you must separate from my house,' he told me, so I could not become a Christian. But last year, my father died so now I can take water baptism in Jesus' name. My father died last year. Praise the Lord." "Due to my father's having already died, I can take water baptism in Jesus' name. Praise the Lord! Praise the Lord!"

West Bengal

He also related, "When we apply the name of Jesus, mosquitoes cannot enter my house. We do not need mosquito nets. They fear the name of Jesus." I had never heard of this, and though I am a pastor, I have never experienced anything like this.

That whole area is full of monkeys. I was asked, "Pastor, do you want to eat one of these monkeys?"

"Oh, if you can kill one, this will be a first-class monkey for me." We tried to kill one, but we had no guns. We tried to stone them, but we couldn't.

When I told Brother Danishka, a pastor from Nagaland, about this, he said, "Oh, pastor, if you are going back, please inform me. I will take my guns. Then we shall kill monkeys and carry them back to our homes."

Lera

FOREIGN VISITORS

At the 1975 Northeast Indian general conference, left to right: Lerthansung, J. O. and Mary Wallace, Thansanga.

Presenting Sister Paul Cook, wife of the regional field supervisor, with a gift.

21 (1983-1986)

Bhutan

The predominantly Buddhist country of Bhutan is on the northeast border of India, and it touches West Bengal State. There is a big town there, which we call Gumtu. A pastor invited me there when I was in West Bengal, so Pastor Christopher and I went to Bhutan.

The pastor belonged to the Baptist mission. He rented a big house and invited me to have a Bible seminar. I gave him a tract called wheel of prophecy. He was very happy.

When we had the Bible seminar in his house, once I spoke a little bit loudly, and he told me, "Pastor, no need to speak loudly. There are many CID [Criminal Investigation Department] here. If they know that we have a Bible seminar, then you will not get back to India. They will put you in jail."

The pastor completely accepted our truth. He told me, "If I take water baptism next month, they will drop my pay. I get three hundred rupees per month. If they drop my pay, what shall I eat?"

If I had power in myself, I would have promised him,

"We will continue your help." Instead I replied, "I want to promise you, but I do not have the authority. So I have a great burden."

He said, "Though I did not take water baptism in Jesus' name, yet I know this is true. I am a pastor, so if I have candidates for baptism, I do not want to baptize them in the name of the Father, Son and Holy Ghost. I will baptize them in the name of Jesus. What do you think?"

"Ah, it is better to be baptized in Jesus' name. If you do not take water baptism yourself, it is not so nice. If you want to baptize in Jesus' name, you should take it yourself."

I had no time to meet him again. I left some English copies of *Rightly Dividing the Word of Truth*. Brother Christopher distributed them to West Bengal and to Bhutan also. There is another sizeable town under the Bhutan government, and he left some books there, too.

After some months, in 1983 I received a letter from a chief engineer in Bhutan. "Brother Lerthansung, we want to become Christians, but we cannot join an organization because our government is very, very strict. If you can come to Gumtu, then we want to take water baptism in Jesus' name."

I went to a big cement factory there. Small boys worked there, carrying heavy loads.

When I reached my friends, I was very happy. "Praise the Lord! Hallelujah!"

"Please keep quiet. There are many CID."

They fixed food and closed all the doors; then we had food. Then the engineer gave his testimony. "When I was in Darjeeling Mission School, they gave me a Holy Bible.

I was very angry. I thought, I am a Buddhist young man. Why did they give me this Holy Bible? I destroyed it; I put it in a fire. I was a *pukka* [genuine, stalwart] Buddhist young man. After I finished college, I became an engineer, but I had no peace. I tried to find peace, but one night I saw an angel. The angel said, 'There is no peace in the world. You can look many places, but you cannot find it. Yet it is contained in the Holy Bible, which you threw away when you were in high school. If you can find another Bible, it will tell you the way to peace.'

"But I had no Bible. What was I to do? I went back to Darjeeling to the mission's book room and purchased a Scofield Bible for 250 rupees. I spent lots of money. Then, I studied it from Genesis to Revelation. I have read it many times, so I already accept that this is true. From my heart I have already accepted it. Now I have become a Christian."

I told him frankly, "No, no, you did not become a Christian. You *want* to become a Christian. You accepted, but you did not obey. Acceptance and obedience are quite different. You accepted the truth, but until you obey this truth you cannot become a Christian. So you accept Jesus' death for your sin?"

"Yes, yes."

"If you accept, then you must die and be buried with Him by baptism."

"No, I believe, I believe."

"Yes, I think you believe, but acceptance and obedience are a little different. If you accept Jesus' death, you must also die with Him by repentance. You have accepted Jesus' burial in a grave, but You must be buried with Him by baptism in His name. If you accept His resurrection, you must also receive the Holy Spirit. Then you will be a Christian, having identified with the gospel of Christ. Many people when they write their names say, "I am a Christian," but this is not good enough. For true Christianity, you need to repent, you need to be baptized in Jesus' name, and you need to receive the Holy Spirit. This is how to be a real Christian."

"Yes, yes," he said. "I will take water baptism."

That day, we had twelve candidates who wanted to take water baptism. I told them, "If we have baptismal services inside of Bhutan, I will not go back to Shillong because I will go to jail. It is not so far from your place to Brother Christopher's place. I will be watching for you there. Please come down to India."

On Sunday six people came, but the other six could not come because their families were greatly opposed. Six people took water baptism in Jesus' name.

So we have six people in Bhutan, but they say they cannot form an organization because the government is very strict. "We are the underground UPC."

"Yes, yes. The most important thing is that first you must repent and be baptized in Jesus' name and receive the Holy Spirit. God will arrange the rest somehow." The time will come when we will start the UPC in Bhutan somehow.

I am very happy because a general officer told me secretly, "When we had the All-Bhutan Student Union Conference, we made a secret resolution. In comparing Christian lands and non-Christian lands, we find that they are quite different. All the Christian lands physically and spiritually have progressed so much, but the non-Christian lands have not progressed. We in Bhutan are under the

Buddhists, so we are very, very backward. When we become Christians, then Bhutan will progress. Thus we secretly resolved.

Our king wants to become a Christian, because he was brought up in England. But our monks are very strict. For that reason, he cannot say anything. After ten years, the Buddhist priests who are holding us back will have expired, we hope. After they die, the young people, when they take charge, will try to become Chistians.

This is the great expectation for Bhutan. If Jesus does not come, after ten years we have a great hope that Bhutan will also become a Christian land and we will be able to preach the full gospel freely.

After I left Brother Christopher wrote to me that he had baptized two or three people from Bhutan. This is the condition of Bhutan. Though we cannot start the work, though we could not really work, still we have some representatives. And since that's true, it means that we can reach Bhutan with our full gospel.

Lera

Tibetan cottage industry of rug weaving in Pokhara, Nepal.

22 (1984-1986)

Nepal

In 1984 we started a work in the country of Nepal, which is on India's northern border. We had been talking much about Nepal, but we had not had time to visit. Meanwhile God called Brother Lalzuithanga. In his dream he saw a big man who told him to go to Nepal, but he did not want to obey. The third time the big man said, "If you will not go, I will kill you." This he couldn't tolerate.

"I'll go," he promised. He came to our headquarters. "I don't know where I shall go. I know only Nepal. I don't know the name of the city or town where God wants me to go. I'll go. If I don't go, I'll die, so I need to go."

"We'll pray for you." We prayed for him, then he went to Siliguri. From Siliguri he went directly to Pokhara City.

Fortunately, in Pokhara lived some people who had come to Lunglei, Mizoram, as shopkeepers. He knew them, so he stayed with them. First he visited—roaming and traveling—he did not know what to do.

At last he found a group and started to talk to them

Lera

about the full gospel. They accepted and he baptized some people.

[This sounds easier than it actually was, as is usually the case in Northeast Indian understatement. Brother Lalzuithanga objected to the angel that he knew none of the Nepali language. After he went to Nepal, he had services in the home of a family which had faithfully supported their local church and even given land for the church building, until in a church dispute the family was forced out. In these home meetings, Brother Lalzuithanga struggled to preach with a mixture of Hindi, Assamese, and the little bit of Nepali that he had picked up since his arrival.

A few of the people attending the house meetings decided that Brother Lalzuithanga was preaching false doctrine. "Let's beat him," they cried, but the host family said, "No, this is our home. He can preach here if he wants until we can understand what he's trying to say. If you don't want to come, you don't have to, but since this is our home, he stays." He stayed and preached and got through the language barriers.]

Brother Lalzuithanga came back with three friends from Nepal. Later the same big person appeared to him again in a dream and told him to go back. According to his dream, he went back to Nepal. This time he reported that he baptized about seventeen people. They formed the UPC organization with about thirty-five constituents according to his report. The church elders offered him plots of land for a church building.

I instructed him, "Try to register in the name of the United Pentecostal Church. If you can register, then you can appeal to the headquarters for a church building."

Nepal

This is the situation in Nepal.

Fortunately, in 1986 Brother Stanley Scism and Brother Nathan Paul were able to visit Nepal and have a good baptismal service there. We appreciate our first missionary visit to that area.

Many people love Nepal, pray for Nepal, and love to give for Nepal. I am so glad that Brother Stanley Scism and Brother Nathan Paul visited and were burdened. God will never forget this.

Members of the UPC in Nepal standing on the ground they donated for a church.

23 (1986)
Arunachal Pradesh

After that we had a great burden for Arunachal Pradesh, a state in India's extreme northeast on the China border. In previous times we called this place "Satan's bill" because the people there burned down many church buildings, which were costly to replace. The Northeast Indian Christians once had a procession to protest because the people in Arunachal had burned down church buildings and expelled some Christians from their homes. Every denomination participated.

I had a great burden for that area, but I had no time to visit. In January 1986 a sister was working in Arunachal in a wonderful town. In her childhood, she had been brought up in Mizoram because her father was then working in the Assam Rifles. She stayed with her father in Mizoram about five years. During that time she received the Holy Spirit and was baptized in Jesus' name.

By the time she went back to her part of the country, she had forgotten the language. She tried to relearn the language, and God helped her much. After she could

Lera

speak the language, she started to witness in every village. When the people heard she was a Christian, sometimes they kicked her out from their villages. Many times she slept in the jungle. Her mother and her two brothers didn't help her either, for if they helped, then their tribal ruler would not be happy.

However, through her message some people wanted to take water baptism. She had fourteen candidates. Then she wrote to me. In the Mizo language we called her Zoramthari, but in her original language her name is Kenter Doze.

To go I needed to get an inner line permit, so I contacted the liaison officer in the secretariat. He gave me only seven days, for this is a very, very strict area. When I got the seven-day inner line permit, I went to the headquarters town of Along District, which is very near the China border.

When I met the lady, she told me, "I received your letter a little late, so I wrote to those who want to take water baptism. We will try to meet them in their village."

In the first village, our sister had two men to baptize. We went to Pangkhiang Village, but they had not received her letter, so the people who wanted to take water baptism could not come. The next day we planned to pass into another village. We had already purchased tickets and entered into the bus, and the bus had already started, when at that moment a man came with his bag. He wore Nepali dress. "I want to see the pastor, I want to see the pastor."

"I don't know what pastor you want to see. I am the pastor who came from Shillong."

"Yes, yes, you are the one. We received your letter

Arunachal Pradesh

from Sister Zoramthari. We want to take water baptism in our village. Our people do not want to come to this place. They need you to come to our place. If you can come, then we will arrange a big feast."

I asked Sister Zoramthari, "How far is it from here?"

She replied, "Oh, since you are a little old, I don't know if you could go there. That place is about twelve miles. You must go down, down, down, then up, up, up. It is up and down, and the road is very bad." (Coming from her, that meant a lot; in that area of the country, it meant that the road practically disappeared and that the traveler is left to brave the mountains on his own.)

I was thinking, If we hadn't already purchased these tickets, I would want to go, but we already have tickets, so we must make another plan for them. (In India, getting refunds is less common than miracles of healing.) I told the old man, "Old man, please excuse me. By this time we have already purchased our bus tickets. We cannot come. God will arrange the next time. Then I will try to come."

"Yes, yes." He was very happy. "When you come, we shall have a great feast. We have a big pig," he said.

"Yes, yes." Then we started from Pangkhieng to Boleng Village. Boleng is very near the China border. Boleng District is on the eastern side of the Bramaputra River. We could see that the tops of the hills were all covered by snow. It is very cold there. When we reached the village, we stayed with a Mizo family. That night we had a meeting. The people had never seen any other Mizo visitors. Since we were the first, those Mizo people were very happy.

Our host was so happy to see us that he invited peo-

Lera

ple who were working with them, some foresters and some rangers working in the forest, to hear our message. "A pastor arrived from Shillong. He will preach a sermon, so please come, please come!"

I preached in Mizo. Sister Zoramthari translated into their language. After the church meeting, we had a discussion. The people had never heard about Christianity. They had only heard the name "Christians," but they did not know what Christians believed. When we had our discussion, they wanted to accept baptism in Jesus' name.

The next day we went down to the river and had a baptismal service. When we started the worship I felt very happy. I started clapping and saying, "Praise the Lord, praise the Lord, praise the Lord!" My watch fell down, broken, but I didn't care because we were having a baptismal service in a new area. Seven people took water baptism, including a forester and his wife.

"If we become Christians, how shall we pray?" they asked.

"If you are going to take food, you should say, 'Lord Jesus, you have given me this food. We are very happy. Please sanctify it for our bodies. In Jesus' name.'"

"What is another kind of prayer?"

"When you are going to sleep, you will pray like this: 'Lord, I am going to bed. While I am sleeping, I need your help to keep my life. My body I commit into your hand.'"

"When we go to church service, what shall we say?"

"When I reach Shillong, I will write down the keys to prayer. I will write a letter to you."

When I preached the gospel I stated, "In Revelation also we find—"

"What is Revelation?" they wanted to know. They

had never heard of Revelation. When they heard "Revelation says. . ." they asked, "Is Revelation a person?"

"No, no, no, the name of a book." The names of the Bible they had never heard. It was very, very difficult to preach.

"We need to find out what to do."

"Don't worry. I also know you need Bibles. I will report to headquarters."

When I came back to Shillong, I wrote a letter to Lunglei, Mizoram, since Sister Zoramthari had been brought up in that district. When they received my letter, the believers in Lunglei sent Rs 390. We were able to purchase three English Bibles and one Mizo Bible. The sister could read only Mizo. Her Bible was a very old edition, so we purchased a new one. I appointed a secretary and treasurer for the new church.

The church in Arunachal has appointed Brother Panor to come to Shillong for Bible school. They know very little about the Christian teaching, but whatever we say they accept. For this reason we must be very, very careful.

In that area I purchased a pair of canvas shoes made in China. Unfortunately, they were too small.

Some years back, the family of T. Ezing, who was working as field publicity officer, came to Shillong from Arunachal. I baptized the whole family. There we also have an opening, but I don't know their address.

Wangcho, a sewing instructor in West Siang, a district in Arunachal, wrote a letter to me. "Brother Lerthansung, please come to West Siang. I will fly by helicopter, then we shall meet together in the Kusum Hotel." I went there to West Siang and we met together in the Kusum Hotel. He rented a room for one hundred rupees. In the early morning we woke up and at 5:30 we had a baptismal service in the Bramaputra River. Many people were taking baths and doing other things, but he and I had a baptismal service.

At seven AM he flew back to his home area. He told me, "My wife wanted to come, but since we had no money, we could not come together."

I felt a great pain in my heart. If I had had money, I would have offered to send the money for her fare, but I could not make such a promise. That day I would have liked very much to become rich.

God has used Sister Zoramthari in a very mighty way. One lady was going to die. The doctors gave her no hope. They said to her husband, "Your wife has no hope. Take her back to your home before she dies." The husband began crying and crying.

At that time Sister Zoramthari visited the hospital. She told the husband, "I want to pray for her healing."

"Oh, pray, pray," he said. She did.

One morning the lady began to sit up and eat well. After three days she could walk nicely. Four days later she returned to their home.

When the people saw this they and the village chief said, "Other Christian pastors cannot come to our village. We have a sister who can pray for sick people. Zoramthari is enough." Only when they heard about this miracle would their chief accept her. Now she is free to witness in the village.

Because of her ministry and faithfulness the mission executive board appointed her as an evangelist and sends two hundred rupees per month for her travel allowance. She received a Bible woman certificate in 1986. (In India, women do not get local, general or ordination licenses; instead, they can receive Bible woman certificates.) She's a small girl.

By the beginning of 1986 we had eleven people who took water baptism in Arunachal. By the help of God, our full gospel is going on to some people who have received Bibles, and one fellow will come to Bible school. We will train him, and when he goes back, we will appoint him as pastor. When he has finished his Bible course, then we will not need to go ourselves. It's a very, very strict area. Even now in that part of the country people still burn down church buildings. It is very, very difficult to preach there.

For me to go back to Arunachal is difficult. When I stayed in the headquarters town of West Siang District, two times the CID (Criminal Investigation Department) came to my place. "Who are you?"

"I am Lerthansung." I did not want to say "Reverend" or "Pastor." I simply said my name.

"Where are you from?"

"Shillong." They asked more questions, but I didn't want to say anything about religious work. I simply said, "I am a tourist in Arunachal." The area is very, very strict so we have to be careful.

I returned to Arunachal in 1986 and baptized eight more people. Some of the people had heard of the Bible but had never seen one. When I showed them my Bible they were very happy. I have great hope for that area.

Lera

Lerthansung arrayed in Arunachal splendor with saints from that area. The lady is Kenter Doze (Zoramthari). She is about twenty-one.

24 (1984-1986)

Calcutta

I had a great burden for Calcutta, the capital of West Bengal State, for many years. The UPC work there began during the time of Brother E. L. Scism, our former superintendent, but the minister who first worked there was not capable, according to the report of Brother Harry Scism. We never had a preaching point. Due to our leader, our work was spoiled. For a long time we had no preaching point.

[Some additional information from E. L. Scism: originally, the Oneness message was brought to Calcutta by Brother and Sister Buck. Brother Buck was a dentist missionary who later died working in Hong Kong. He worked with C. T. Studd and is mentioned in the latter's book. Once in Calcutta, Brother E. L. Scism was with the Bucks in a day service with their small group in Calcutta. Later, Brother Buck recommended a certain young man as a worker for Calcutta. When Brother Harry Scism went to check up on him at his place of work, it turned out that the young man had been contacting the UPC under an assumed name as an alleged convert from Islam. He was, however, still Islamic posing as a Moslem in order to work for the Urdu newspaper. When Brother Harry found him in a park, he was smoking and tried to hide his cigarette behind his back, but the smoke trailed up behind his back. Neither the man's co-workers at his job nor in the church appreciated his duplicity. He was, of course, immediately disfellowshiped.]

I thought, We need to start the work, but the greatest difficulty for us is that in Calcutta the rent is very high. I wanted to appeal to the international headquarters. I talked to Brother Harry Scism, then I talked to Brother Cook also. "If you can rent a building in Calcutta, then we shall give monthly help from Northeast India. We must work together from America and from Northeast India."

Brother Cook agreed and helped me. He appealed to Brother Kilgore's church in Houston, Texas, and they were also burdened for Calcutta city. They agreed. "We shall help for the rent in Calcutta city."

The Northeast Indian church passed a resolution to help, and we began to make arrangements. Our first question was, Who could we send? If we appointed one of the Bengali people, according to Brother Harry Scism, we needed to be careful because they are very, very wise people.

For some time we planned to appoint a certain Bengali, but first we wanted a chance to hear him preach. We decided, We will invite him to come up to the general conference and give him a chance to speak. We shall listen to his sermon. If it is a powerful sermon, we shall arrange to appoint him. When he came to attend our general conference in Aizawl we gave him a chance. His message had no power at all. It was not a Pentecostal message. He preached a message like the pastors of other churches. The executive board members were not happy. "We do not want to appoint him. His sermon is completely dead."

What could we do? At that moment Brother Nathan Paul came to our UPC. He had a big church position; he looked after Meghalaya and Assam states for his mission. According to his report, under him were 150 churches. He accepted the truth and was baptized in Jesus' name. Because of the truth he had to resign his position and leave his house.

[One of the primary causes for his conversion was Sister Satinvela. Brother Nathan Paul was walking along the road when he saw our headquarters church building with its sign on which the name of Jesus only is written in big letters. Upset because "they left out the Father and the Holy Ghost," he walked in to tell somebody off. He met our superintendent's wife, who invited him to tea and asked if he had been baptized in Jesus' name. Angered at what he considered an insult to his ecclesiastical dignity, he stormed out. At home, he had time to think about what she had said. He came back shortly afterward and in contrition asked to be baptized in the name of Jesus.]

After Brother Nathan Paul took water baptism in Jesus' name, Brother Kilgore met him in Madras and liked him very much. He told me, "Brother Lerthansung, you can appoint him."

"But we do not want to appoint him immediately. We have never heard about him before. When we go back to Shillong, we must inquire from his old church as to his condition. If he has no bad condition, we shall appoint him."

Lera

When we went back to Shillong, Brother Chunga and I went to his church and met the assistant pastor. The assistant pastor asked, "Who are you?"

"We are pastors Chunga and Lerthansung." (We did not want to say "Pentecostal church.") "We want to invite Brother Nathan Paul, your pastor. We've heard about him, but we've never met him personally. We want to have a revival meeting, so if possible we want to invite him for our speaker, but we don't know what preaching position he has."

"As far as I know, he's a top preacher. Nathan Paul is the best preacher. I like him very much, but I'm very sorry that since the month of February he fell into bad doctrine. We had a discussion with him, but we could not change him. We reported to our headquarters. Our headquarters sent a strong letter asking what false doctrine he had. We explained, 'He believes in only one God. And he exalts baptism in Jesus' name.' Headquarters responded, 'Baptism in Jesus name? We never heard of this. This is a false doctrine.' We believe in the trinity, but he believes in one true God. We are very sorry. What to do? We cannot convince him otherwise," the pastor concluded.

Brother Chunga and I were very happy inside, but we did not want to laugh before him. What he called a bad point was a good point for us. We reported to the executive board, and the executive board appointed him as Calcutta pastor.

Before we appointed Nathan Paul, the executive board had appointed me to start the work in Calcutta. "You must move to Calcutta with your family. When you get a capable person, you can return to Shillong. We have already decided." Just before I moved, we found Nathan Paul. We appointed him, but the executive board wanted me still. "He is a new person for us. Though he has accepted the one true God, though he took water baptism in Jesus' name, you need to help him start the work, so you need to move for the time being to Calcutta with your wife."

So my wife and I moved to Calcutta for the time being and helped Nathan Paul. When we started the work, God blessed us. After one week, we had a baptismal service in Hooghly River. Nine people took water baptism in Jesus' name.

At that time, one Bengali said, "I feel a great touch in my heart. Hamar Jesu, amir ki kari bu; hamar Jesu, amir ki kari bu." That means, "Lord Jesus, what shall I do? Lord Jesus, what shall I do?" He felt the Holy Spirit.

That place is called Batanagar. After Batanagar, we started a work in the Tutanagar area also. So in Calcutta we now have two preaching points. In another suburb also we have great hope, but at this time we do not have a preaching point there. Some day we hope to have a good church there, too.

God has helped Brother Nathan Paul mightily. There was a crippled boy, more than twelve years old, who had never walked. The Bengali people challenged Brother Nathan Paul. "If you can heal this cripple, then we shall believe your doctrine." They challenged him in the Howrah section, the western side of the city.

Brother Nathan Paul prayed for the cripple. After he prayed he commanded. "Straighten! In the name of Jesus!" The crippled boy began to walk straight. Now he walks all right.

Lera

Then those people said, "Nathan Paul's doctrine is good," but they did not want to obey. Yet, I have great hope for Howrah also.

When they heard that we had started the United Pentecostal Church, the Victory Church and other churches combined to publish a paper that announced, "Nathan Paul is UPC. The UPC is a bad organization. The World Council of Churches does not accept them. They have bad doctrine." In some places people tried to kill Brother Nathan Paul. But God helped him. They did not kill him and he continued his work.

Fortunately, some missionaries were able to visit. When one of them visited Calcutta and saw the condition of Brother Nathan Paul, he so loved him that he gave him a motorcycle. Brother Nathan Paul did not want to register it personally so he sent it to the church. We registered it in the name of the United Pentecostal Church. That brother I've never met, but I love him very much.

In Calcutta we have great hope to extend the work of God.

25 (1985-1986)
Garo Hills

According to the Bible, if we sow the seed then we shall reap. After we started in Calcutta, we tried to have another beginning—the Garo Hills.

The Garo Hills is a separate district. Because of a political freedom movement, the Khasi Hills and the Garo Hills were combined into the one state of Meghalaya. Garo Hills is near Bangladesh. The people are Garo—tribal people. Though we were in Shillong, the capital of Meghalaya, we never visited it. It is about 180 miles away.

In 1985 I received message from Tripura that a sick person suffering from cancer had come to Hmarkolien. He wanted to hear our message, so he sent a friend. "I want to hear a message from Brother Lerthansung. While he was in Lakhipur then I met him. We talked together about the full gospel." He was very interested.

When he reached Tura, the capital of the Garo Hills, he wrote a letter to me. "Brother Lerthansung, if you could spare time, please come to the Garo Hills. We want to hear your message." Pastor Ngurchuaia and I went.

Lera

When we reached Tura, nobody knew me. I also did not know a single person—only that sick man.

The sick man was an educated person. His wife worked in the employment office.

They rented a big hall. Every night they paid thirty-five rupees. They said, "We will take the responsibility. We shall rent for one week for your preaching. Money's nothing." They were very happy. They invited many people. "Brother Lerthansung came from Shillong. He's a Pentecostal pastor. He's going to preach the sermon in Bonepa Hall."

At the first meeting we had four people. I preached as best I could. We were very happy. The next night more than twenty people gathered together. By the last service the hall was totally full.

Saturday night I appealed to the people. "Now you have already heard about the one true God. You have already heard the full gospel. But simply hearing is not enough. It cannot save you if you do not obey the truth. For those who want to obey the truth, tomorrow we will have a baptismal service." Then I prayed for them. We had seventeen candidates.

Of the seventeen candidates, twelve were women and five were men, but there was one sub-inspector of police present, a Mizo. He came to me. "Brother Lerthansung, don't worry about having more women than men. Their custom is this: the family is controlled by the woman. The husband has no authority. If the husband wants to go to sleep before the wife orders, the husband cannot sleep. When they hear from their wife, 'Please come here. Please lie down,' then they can sleep. Also, if the wife does not order, the husband cannot take food. So, if you can convince twelve women, you can convince twelve houses."

That was the first baptismal service. After two months they invited me again. I went to many services.

Those who had taken water baptism wanted to redo their legal marriage. They all wanted to marry with a Christian marriage license. That day they invited all the educated people and all the officers, because one candidate's mother was deputy speaker in the Meghalaya government. She was a big official. She said to me, "Brother Lerthansung, there's no need to say so much about marriage in your sermon. People want to hear about the one true God and baptism in Jesus' name."

"Yes, yes." So, although we were gathering together for the sake of the marriage service, I preached about the one true God and baptism in Jesus' name. At last, I took up the point of the marriage service. After the marriage service, we had a great feast.

After the feast, the deputy speaker invited all the people. "Brother Lerthansung is a Pentecostal pastor. I like him very much. He graduated from a trinity Bible school, and he graduated from a true Bible school also. You can ask him anything." Then we had a discussion.

The next day five people took water baptism. That day, I asked some officials, "Why, after you know the truth, you do not take water baptism? You must take water baptism."

But the two officials replied, "Pastor, the United Pentecostal Church is a new organization for us. All the organizations have cemeteries, but the UPC has none. Suppose that before we obtain a cemetery, we die. What shall we do? We accept your message, but if we join the UPC, and die before we have a cemetery, the other mis-

Lera

sions will not allow us to be buried in their cemetery. They each decided on a big plot to purchase for a cemetery. So, after we purchase a cemetery, we will take water baptism."

In the first week of January 1986, I went back to the Garo Hills. Some pastors had wanted to have a marriage service. The groom's father was a rich person, and he prepared a big *pandal* (brush arbor). We had the marriage service there.

From Tura in six jeeps, two cars, and one full bus we went there. More than three thousand people gathered together. The deputy speaker said to me, "Brother Lerthansung, as you spoke before, you need not say too much about the people to be married. These people need to hear about the one true God and baptism in Jesus' name."

I started from Genesis. "In the beginning God created the heaven and the earth. He made Adam. Adam was alone. He had no helper, so God made Eve. Then they were married together. So marriage services are God ordained. The God who created heaven and earth and who made Adam is Jesus. You may wonder about this, but I will explain it to you. In the beginning, God created heaven and earth according to Genesis 1:1. In Revelation 1:8 we see that it was Jesus who laid the foundation of the earth. So the woman and Adam were united in Jesus."
Thus I compared the Scriptures. Since I was a new person, all the people kept looking.

"According to the Book of Colossians, Jesus is the name of our God. For that reason, Paul wrote, 'Whatever you do, do in the name of Jesus'. We need not say many things, except that, first, the name of Jesus is very important and, second, you need to take water baptism in Jesus' name. What for? For the remission of your sins." Then I explained that.

They had never heard a message like this. "It is very wonderful," they said. But the people were not theologians, so whatsoever I said they wanted to accept.

After we had a baptismal service, we went back to Tura. The people who were church leaders in the village said, "If you can come to our village, we want to hear a message from you."

I told them frankly, "When you become Christians and after some years with the Mizo people, then you will be real Christians. You ordered in Christianity, but you did not receive the revival movement, even though your condition is very poor. The most important thing is revival, the outpouring of the Holy Ghost." They had never heard about the revival movement.

Since we have a UPC in Tura and the people who are members of our UPC are educated people, through them we can progress to other things also. I have great hope.

Anyhow, we started the work in Tura. According to our UPC jurisdiction, it is geographically in the Central District. We have mission works in Calcutta, Andaman, West Bengal, Darjeeling, Sikkim, Nepal, Arunachal, and Tura, in addition to the works under our districts. We have eight district headquarters; these others are mission fields.

Lera

This Riang family was baptized by Thangliana, missions director in North Mizoram.

26 (1985-1986)

South Tripura

In 1985 we passed a resolution to evangelize South Tripura near the Bangladesh border. The people there are called the Riang. The Riang people are very backward. They are not completely naked, but otherwise they are like the naked people.

Now we have twelve preaching points there. All the educated people and all the high school students have become Christians. Their parents say, "If we send our children to school, they will become Christian. It is not good." In other words, the Indian students say the same thing as the Bhutanese: "Our fathers and the old men—when they die, all South Tripura will become a Christian country."

Our mission director there, Santirai Riang, has a B.A. and graduated with honors. Our secretary, Moyuk Sangma, has an M.A. Our treasurer, Upendra Riang, has a B.A. One of our sisters, Sangi, is a supervisor. So all our church board in Tripura are educated persons.

From South Tripura to the district headquarters of

Lera

Tripura is very far—more than two hundred miles. For that reason the Tripura District is very difficult to look after. Also, since others in Tripura cannot speak the Riang language, we had to conduct the district meetings in English.

But it is very difficult for the Tripura pastors to have English services, so they handed over the Riang area to the General Missions Department. "It is impossible for us to look after them. It's better to put them under the missions department because you can help all the workers from the General Missions Department."

In Tripura we have good preaching points now. We have eight churches. When we visit Tripura, it is a wonderful thing. When they see me they say, "Oh, the pastor is coming!" Then they go to the church and ring the bell. They never think, It's two o'clock, or it's six o'clock. They go to their church and ring the bell for service, regardless of the time of day.

They knew only two gospel songs. They'd start one song. When they finished, they'd sing the other. They translated Mizo songs and gave me a copy. I typed them, then sent them back to their director. "Director, please correct my typing. I cannot understand your language. Is it correct or not, my typing? Please correct it. When you correct it, I will cut a stencil. Then you can have many songs." When I came back to Tripura, they gave me about fifty songs to duplicate.

It's so very difficult to have a song service when you have only two songs. They learned some English songs, but they did not know the meaning of the words. Then the former pastor taught them Mizo songs like, "Aw Kalvary thing chungah chuan ka hreng ropui a au." They could sing them, but they did not know the meaning. Still, they were Christian songs, so they loved them.

27 (1985)
The Philippines, Japan, and Thailand

In March 1955 God let me see a great vision. In that vision, God made me tour the countries of Japan and Thailand. From that vision I gave my heart to Japan and Thailand. The thought came to me that one day I would either go and preach the gospel or would be a missionary to these countries.

In 1980 Brother Fujibayashi, then superintendent of Japan, came to Shillong, and there I told him of my tour of Japan and Thailand in my vision. I even wrote to him in a letter that one day God would make a way for me to visit Japan. From my position, I could never hope to go to Japan, but in 1984 the General Missions Board recommended that I attend the third world conference, which was to be held in Manila. The recommendation made by the General Missions Board was approved and accepted by the General Executive Board of Northeast India. "Moved by Reverend K. Darsailova and seconded by Reverend K. Ropara that Reverend Lerthansung be sent to the world conference in Manila in addition to the national representative as per the General Missions Board resolution. . . .They will be allowed to visit the church in Asia."

I responded, "Oh, I have no objection. Wherever you want me to go, I'm going."

The American missionary board accepted and approved the resolution to send our superintendent and me to Manila. The General Executive Board of Northeast India further permitted us to visit several important UPC headquarters in Asia after the Manila conference. I was very happy.

We bought our air tickets through the Calcutta Travel Corporation of India. While we were getting the tickets for Japan, I suddenly remembered the vision from God I had seen in 1955 and realized that God was now fulfilling it. Although there is much to write about my journey, yet it is enough to say that God fulfilled my vision of 1955 after thirty years. Praise the Lord!

The will and choice of God and man are not always the same, so to those who see visions it is important to know the timing in the will of God. Those who try to conduct themselves according to their own choices only bring weakness, so in everything we do and in all our ways we must always wait patiently for the true voice of God.

After we had gotten visas for the Philippines and the other countries and had booked our tickets, I went down to Calcutta with our superintendent, Brother Satinvela. Before we went Brother Hnezova, our general treasurer, sent eight thousand rupees for our traveler's checks. I don't know the reason, but after one month the exchange

Philippines, Japan, Thailand

office had still not received our money. If we could purchase the traveler's checks, then we could exchange money easily, but since the office hadn't received our money, there was some trouble. We did not know what to do.

Then I told Brother Satinvela, "I have a good friend who is a financial secretary for the Salvation Army. We shall borrow from him about eight thousand, then we shall pay him tomorrow. When we ring up Brother Hnezova by telephone, tell him to bring the money tomorrow."

We woke up early the next morning to book a telephone call to Brother Hnezova. Brother Hnezova picked up our call. "Yes, yes. I will come tomorrow. Don't worry. I will bring money."

If he came by airbus, he would reach Calcutta about 4:00 PM. By that time the exchange office would have closed. The day after that we needed to leave. We were very troubled. "Anyhow, let's go to the Salvation Army headquarters," we decided.

The next day we went to the Salvation Army headquarters and met Brother Sangzuala. He was my best friend while I was in Cachar. "We need your help. Our treasurer will be arriving this evening. He will bring money. But today we need to exchange our money. Please give us eight thousand rupees from your Salvation Army funds."

"Brother, if you need only three thousand, I can give it to you from my pocket. But eight thousand is a lot of money. If I give it you from our accounts, this is not according to the rules. For that I have no authority at all, so it's better to meet our top officer."

I went to the top officer. First I complimented him

much. "Oh, brother, I heard that you visited Mizoram. I am very happy."

He greeted me in Mizo, "Chibai, chibai, chibai." He could speak in Mizo only "Chibai."

"All our Mizo people love you very much. When you came to Mizoram all our Mizo section was very happy. 'This is a good leader,' they say."

"What do you want?"

"Oh, sir, tomorrow we are going to Bangkok. Today our treasurer will reach Calcutta at 4:00 PM. He will bring our money. This money we already arranged by trunk call. But today we need to purchase our foreign exchange. What to do? So let me borrow eight thousand rupees."

He called another officer. "This brother needs eight thousand rupees. For this kind of thing we have no rule. What to do? Still, I know very well that he needs it. If they do not exchange their money now, tomorrow it will be impossible."

"What to do? What to do?" they asked one another.

My friend, the financial secretary, spoke up. "Ah, please give it to him. No harm. Their secretary will arrive this evening. I believe this man. I trust him very much. You need not write a letter. We shall give it to him, then we shall receive it back tomorrow."

Then the top officer replied, "Yes, yes. Since we are working together for the Lord, we need not make so much trouble. Give, give."

He gave me eight thousand rupees. Brother Satinvela and I went to the Reserve Bank and purchased traveler's checks. That evening, Brother Hnezova arrived in Calcutta.

Early in the morning, before we went to the airport,

Philippines, Japan, Thailand

we went to the Salvation Army headquarters and we gave them back eight thousand rupees. They were very happy.

When we arrived in the airport office, and after we got our boarding pass, we entered into the security room. Although there were other passengers, when the guards saw us they thought that Brother Satinvela and I were foreigners. But when they saw our passports, they realized we were Indian. Then they suspected that we had brought in dollars illegally.

[This sounds typical of many immigration and customs officials. When it becomes obvious that they have made a mistake, they would rather die than admit it, so they involve a technicality or launch an inquisition as absurd as it is aggravating or terrifying, possibly intending that the victim will feel such relief at the cessation of hostilities that he will forget their paranoid incompetence which initiated the entire calamity. Anyway, after a typically futile and misdirected investigation, the customs men were obliged to conclude their persecutions with predictable unproductivity.]

Amid all the investigation Brother Satinvela seemed like Jesus at Calvary. He was like a lamb; he did not say anything. "You must be like Jesus," I told him. He laughed and laughed.

Finally we entered into the waiting room, and from there we boarded the airplane to Bangkok, Thailand.

We never had experienced such things on an airplane. We were sitting in executive class. We did not know executive class tickets from others, but the travel agency, when booking our tickets, reserved expensive tickets in order to receive lots of commission. In all our hotels also they booked two rooms. We had told them to give us a double room, but they booked two rooms. So we spent lots of money because we did not have experience.

The air hostesses did a very good job. First they presented flowers. They dressed nicely and had a very good smell. I told Brother Satinvela, "Oh, Brother Satinvela, these ladies did very well and they also smell very good. I wanted them to stand around more times. I have no objection." He laughed and laughed.

When we landed in Bangkok, we met Brothers J. R. Buai and George Shalm. Then we put up in the same hotel and the next day flew from Bangkok to Manila, Philippines.

When we landed in Manila, before we reached the customs clearing, about ten of our UPC girls stood together. They brought garlands and some pieces of paper. They asked, "Are you a UPC delegate?"

"Yes, yes." Then they gave us garlands.

Those girls were so beautiful. When I saw their dress, I was very happy. Oh, these are real UPC girls, I thought.

They took our passports, cleared us through customs, and sent us to a bus. We went first class. The bus dropped us off at the Philippine Plaza Hotel, our hotel for the conference.

During the conference, we met some of our friends. We were very happy. Brother Scism and Brother T. F. Tenney and other visitors had come from abroad. One night I met Brother Wieteska, who had come from Switzerland. After the church meeting, he came up.

"Brother, I saw you before. Do you know me?"

"Oh, Brother Wieteska, I know you very well. During your honeymoon in Landour, we talked together. When I perform a marriage service, I mention your name to the people: 'Brother Wieteska, when he got married, came to Landour for his honeymoon. Sometimes we played Chinese checkers together. When we were playing, in one day seventy-five times he would kiss his wife. He loves her so much. His wife's name is Lorna, but he never calls her Lorna. He always calls her darling.'"

Brother Wieteska was very happy. He called all the people who had come from Switzerland. "Brother Lerthansung has a prophecy." Then I repeated my story. After the church meeting, he invited me to take a cup of cold drink. At that time he asked, "How can I help you?"

"Oh, if you want to help me, I have many urgent things. When I visit Churachandpur, there is one place very far from our headquarters. The people need a building, but they cannot purchase the land. That land, when I saw it, cost about twenty thousand rupees."

"I cannot promise you twenty thousand, but I will try and do what I can do."

Later the district secretary in Churachandpur told me, "Brother Wieteska wrote to us saying, 'I sent fifteen hundred dollars to the international headquarters for the plot of land.' So we have great hope." Brother Wieteska did very well for our country.

After the Manila conference, we stayed about three days in Manila. Then we traveled with our workers. I had a good chance to speak in one church. When I preached first I said, "When I came to Manila, I thought, I will be a foreigner. But when I saw your face, I thought I had reached my home town. I can say this is my home town." All the people were very happy.

Then we went to Japan. In Japan also we had a

wonderful time preaching the gospel. Brother Satinvela preached in one church; I preached in another.

In some cities we had Bible seminars. Brother Okura informed us, "Most of these people aren't UPC, but when they hear that an Indian pastor will be coming, then they want to see you. So please try to convince these people." After preaching we had a Bible class on the subject "The Old Testament Jehovah in Jesus." I explained it from the Bible. The people were very happy. After we left, some people took water baptism in Jesus' name.

From Japan we went to Hong Kong where we met Brother Forbush and Brother George Shalm. We stayed one night, then we came back from Hong Kong to Bangkok, where we met Brother Chaiyong, the superintendent of Thailand. We purchased some history books and read about some people called Lusei, who live in the Chiangmai District of Thailand near Burma. We are exactly the same as these people—their culture and everything.

After we reached India, Brother Satinvela wrote to Brother Chaiyong, "These people we want to meet. What can we do?"

Brother Chaiyong responded, "I already baptized about one hundred of those people."

In conclusion, during our Manila trip we had great joy and we had a great burden for the work of God in that area. The Japanese people also said, "If you can come back, we will be very grateful." Some people said, "I will give your fare. Our condition is very close. The Americans presented the gospel message to us, but we can relate to you a little easier."

I told them, "Yes, that is right. With America we cannot compare. God arranged for the American people to preach the gospel everywhere, so of course we can say this."

The Manila conference trip made us very, very happy.

Lera

India

28 (1958)
Mainland India I

[This account of Brother Lerthansung's life has followed a roughly chronological pattern, discussing the various areas in India and in neighboring countries in the order in which Brother Lerthansung first visited them. His visits usually resulted in the founding of churches in those areas. The main body of India has been reserved for the last, even though Lerthansung's first contact with the church there was in 1958, because of the immense challenge involved in reaching India's rapidly growing population, which has already passed eight hundred million. At the present rate of growth, India's population will pass China to become the world's most populous nation by 2030.

The church in Northeast India has a great burden to evangelize the rest of India, as witnessed by their efforts in Andaman, West Bengal and Sikkim. They seek a cooperative effort between the two administrative units in India and Northeast India for a united evangelistic effort involving American, Indian, and Northeast Indian resources of finance, workers, and spiritual power. An example and an instigator of this burden in others is Brother Lerthansung, for he plays various roles on the vast and heavily cast center stage of the Indian subcontinent. The following two chapters tell that story, the final act of which has not yet been played.]

Now I am going to report on the first general conference I attended in India. When we had a district conference in Aizawl, Brother E. L. Scism came to Mizoram. At that time he told us that Brother Zakamlova and I needed to come to Adur, Kerala, South India, as representatives from Northeast India. "We are going to have the first general conference for all of India. I already booked your tickets from Silchar to Calcutta by airplane." This was for March 1958.

Brother E. L. Scism purchased our tickets between Silchar and Calcutta. He gave us money for our train fares from Calcutta, and he gave us five hundred rupees for our food on the way. He instructed us on how to reach Calcutta, Madras, and Kerala. We were very happy. Then he left us in Aizawl.

At that time I had never visited the main part of India. This was my first experience, but Brother Zakamlova during the Second World War had joined the Indian Army Medical Corps, the IMCA. He was a pharmacist, so I believed that he had experience.

Brother Zakamlova said, "Brother Lerthansung, if we are going to mainland India...while I was in the military, if we put on military uniforms, then we were very free in the railway system. So we need to put on military uniforms. Then the people will respect us."

I thought, If this is so, then I will purchase a military uniform. So I went to a second-hand store and purchased a military uniform—shirt and pants.

Mainland India I

When I put them in my bag, Brother Zakamlova said, "Please purchase another rucksack. In the military they use rucksacks." Then we went to Silchar, Cachar District, where we met some of our group. Brother Zakamlova told them, "We are going to mainland India for the United Pentecostal Church General Conference."

It is necessary to eat food between Silchar and Calcutta, but we did not know that our air tickets included food. Between Silchar and Calcutta there is one stop, Agartala. In the early morning we flew from Silchar. When we stopped at Agartala Airport, all the passengers deplaned for food, but we did not know the rules. We thought that we needed to pay. Brother Zakamlova told me, "Brother Lerthansung, we are going to a far country, but we have not enough money. Therefore, we cannot take food this time. Instead, it's better to have prayer to God. So, it's OK." We had prayer inside the airplane while the other were having their food.

When the others had finished their food, they came back to the airplane and asked, "Why did you not come for food?"

Brother Zakamlova answered, "We have a small amount, so we did not want to go out."

"No, no, no, you did not need to pay. Our air tickets include all this food." By then we had no time to go out for that food, so we were feeling hungry.

I told Brother Zakamlova, "Since you are older, I thought you would have experience. But since you have no experience, we are hungry. You need not help the government." The airline is a nationalized industry.

When we reached Calcutta, I asked Brother Zakamlova, "Where shall we put up?"

Lera

Brother Zakamlova thought and thought. "I do not know where to put up, but I heard that the Salvation Army has a headquarters. Some of our Mizo people work there. First, it's better to go to the Salvation Army headquarters." We took a taxi. We did not know the exact place. Then Brother Zakamlova said, "Brother Lerthansung, look on the left side. I will look on the right side. Then we can see it." At last we found the Salvation Army headquarters.

When we entered that house, there was one officer from Mizoram. First he welcomed us. "Come in, come in, take rest." However, when he found out that we were going to Kerala for the UPC conference and that we were UPC workers and pastors, he was angry. He thought, This UPC—they have slipped into the Salvation Army headquarters. Finally he told us, "Sorry, you see, we have no room for you. Better go out somewhere."

We were very sorry. We did not know where to go. At last we asked him, "If you have no room for us, we have no objection, but please tell us the names of some Mizo people in Calcutta." Then he wrote down the address of some ladies who were working in a government office.

We took a taxi to Roy Street, Calcutta 16. We got out on Roy Street and searched slowly, slowly, slowly. At last we found the residence of Sister Minnie. She was a nurse working in the military hospital.

When we entered, she was very happy. "Oh, come in, come in. We never see Mizo people in Calcutta. You are our first visitors. Please stay with us for one or two days." Her husband, Brother Muana, was also very kind to us.

Mainland India I

We arrived after their meal, so Brother Zakamlova and I went out for food to Lee Memorial Hotel. We had never heard of menus. In Silchar, when we enter into a hotel, there are no menus. Rice and curry is all there is. When we come in, we ask for chicken curry, fish curry, or mutton curry.

After we entered the hotel, Brother Zakamlova said, "Brother Lerthansung, since you can speak a little Bengali, please tell them that we need a full plate of rice and a full plate of chicken curry." Then I ordered.

They cut the chicken—a half plate plus a whole plate. Brother Zakamlova was so happy. "Since we are UPC pastors we received a great blessing. This kind of food the other people never receive."

They gave us the bill: for one man, seventeen rupees. At that time in Silchar we could get for one rupee a full plate of rice and curry. Here they charged seventeen rupees per plate. Brother Zakamlova was very displeased, so angry. He said to the waiter, "Ah, I think you are mistaken. In Silchar we never give more than one or two rupees. How can you charge for one plate seventeen rupees?"

I went to the manager. "Please explain. In Silchar we never give more than one rupee. How can you charge us seventeen rupees per plate? It is not so good."

But the manager showed us the rate. "You said, 'Full plate chicken curry.' That full plate is sixteen rupees. Your rice is only one rupee, but the chicken is very high, so altogether seventeen rupees."

Brother Zakamlova was angry, but I told him, "You already ate it. What can you do?"

He was still very displeased and said, "Brother Lera

Lera

what shall I do? I've never heard of such a high rate, but we cannot refuse them since we already ate it." Thus we gave Rs 34 for two plates with great sorrow.

Brother Muana was very kind. "If you have never visited Madras, then at Howrah Station in Calcutta you may have trouble. I will come up with you to Howrah Station. Then you can buy tickets for Madras. After I see you off at the Madras Mail, I will go back home." We were happy.

I told Brother Zakamlova, "Though the Salvation Army did not welcome us, God arranged things somehow. This couple was very kind to us. We need not be upset."

But Brother Zakamlova was very angry. "Such kind of people I can never respect, although they are religious leaders. Why do they not want to accept me?"

I told him, "No, no, no. Even among the UPC, there are some revival people and some nonrevival people. Those who have received the Holy Spirit we call revival people. Those who have *not* received the Holy Spirit we call *non*revival people. Since these people are Salvation Army and have not received the Holy Spirit, how can they be happy because we belong to the United Pentecostal Church?"

The next day we went to Howrah Station, then got a train ticket for the Madras Mail. Our brother helped so much.

[Howrah is vast, permeated with pickpockets and full of bedlam. Since this was a few years after partition of India, the problem was even worse then because there was an overflowing refugee camp just outside Howrah.]

We left for Madras on the Madras Mail, third class. It was full of passengers. After two days and two nights,

Mainland India I

we reached Madras Central Station. We did not eat food properly between Calcutta and Madras because we did not know how to get food on a train. From Madras we took another train at Egmore Station for Kerala State.

[Trains from Calcutta to Madras travel on broad gauge rails. Much of South India's travel is by meter-gauge rail. Therefore, a transfer is necessary in Madras from Central Station's broad-gauge to Egmore's meter gauge, or, vice-versa when traveling north. Meter gauge is not very commodious.]

When we got to Kottarakara Station, we went to the bus station and got on the bus. The bus conductor asked, "Where are you going?"

"We are going to Adur. We don't know the exact place. Please help us to go to the right place."

"This bus will go up to Adur. When we stop, you can get out. No need to worry." We were very happy. When we reached Adur, the bus conductor said, "This is Adur. You must get out here."

"Yes, yes." At that time Brother Zakamlova had on his military topcoat. I had on my military long pants and military shirt, but there were no insignia, so the uniform did not help me much. All the people said, "There are many coolies." They thought it was a military uniform, but since there were no insignia they thought, These are poor people.

When we reached Adur, the people wanted to look at us. "Are you coming from Burma? Are you coming from China? Are you coming from Japan?" they asked. But we could not speak together.

Brother Zakamlova said, "Brother Lerthansung, since you are younger than I, talk to them, talk to them.

Lera

I feel tired."

I asked some Keralans, "We want to go to Mission Bungalow. Our missionary's name is E. L. Scism." But when I said "Scism," my pronunciation was quite different than theirs. They could not understand.

"We don't know Scism" they replied. The Malayali people generally say *sissum*. We say *seesm*. They could not understand what we meant.

Meanwhile, many children called out, "Oh, Burmese, Burmese!" We didn't know what to do. If we asked for Mission Bungalow, they did not understand. If we asked where E. L. Seesm was, they did not know.

Then Brother Zakamlova said, "Brother Lerthansung, don't worry. Here is a big street." (It was Main Central, or MC, Street.) "We must go slowly, slowly in this street. God will help us. We could meet someone from the UPC or some other knowledgeable person. Then they can tell us the exact place."

We started to move slowly along that street. Behind us, many children came shouting, "China! China! China!" Some cried "Japanese! Japanese!" Other people said, "Burmese! Burmese! Burmese!" We did not want to stop, because we were very much strangers. The people of Kerala had never seen people who came from Assam (at that time the name for all of Northeast India), so we were very, very strange to them. We roamed around on that road for about three hours.

When we had gone about three to four hundred yards, I saw a sign just above the road: "Repent and be baptized every one of you in the name of Jesus. Then you will receive the Holy Spirit." Then it mentioned Acts 2:38.

I told Brother Zakamlova, "See, here is a beautiful

sign. I will go to this house and ask this houseowner. They will know our missionary, Brother E. L. Scism and his family, if they have such a sign. This sign seems to be our UPC sign."

When I went up to that house, right on MC road, and knocked on the door, a young man opened it. "Who are you?"

"I am Pastor Lerthansung from Manipur, and this is my friend from Mizoram. His name is Reverend Zakamlova. We are of the United Pentecostal Church of India. We are coming for conference. We want to reach Mission Bungalow. Our superintendent is E. L. Scism."

The young man picked up a paper that mentioned our name. "Are you Reverend Lerthansung?" he inquired.

"Yes, yes."

"Are you Reverend Zakamlova?"

"Yes, yes."

"See, this paper they gave me from the headquarters office. Our superintendent, Reverend E. L. Scism, told me that as soon as Brother Zakamlova and Brother Lerthansung arrived, to put them up in this house along with Reverend Harry E. Scism. This house is occupied by Reverend Harry Scism and his wife. I am the cook for them."

Then I told Brother Zakamlova, "Oh, Brother Zakamlova, now we have reached the right place. This is Brother Harry Scism's house. According to their plans, in this house we must stay." As soon as we knew this, we said, "Praise the Lord for guiding us to the very place."

While we were putting up out things, Brother Harry Scism was busy making a *pandal* (brush arbor) at the headquarters.

The young man's name was Victor. He explained, "If you want to take a bath, this is the bathroom. That is your room and there is the dining hall. This is the bath, this is the water pipe, this is the wash place," [sink]. He taught us, and we were very happy.

Brother Zakamlova said to me, "Since we came from Madras, we have had no time to use the bathroom. Let me go first to the bathroom."

After he finished, he pulled a string. Suddenly the water came down. He didn't know what to do. He tried to stop the water, but he couldn't. He called, "Brother Lerthansung, Brother Lerthansung, please come, please come, please come. What happened I don't know. When I pulled down this string, this water came—so much! I did not know what to do. This may be broken." While we were talking, the water completely stopped. This was our first experience in a bathroom. For me it was also very, very convenient to have that experience.

Other experiences we needed. For that reason, I called Brother Victor. He taught us everything. From that day we knew how to operate the bathroom and other rooms as well. We were very, very happy.

During the conference Brother Zakamlova wanted to preach in English. He picked a Bible verse, but sometimes he couldn't express what he felt. Then Brother Zakamlova stood up in the service, "Brother Lera, what shall I do? Can they translate my preaching or not?"

"Brother Zakamlova, don't worry. They can translate. Please go ahead."

While we ate food together, E. L. Scism requested me to take food with them. At that time, T. Samuel was his cook. "Do you want hot curry or *dahl* [lentils]?" he asked.

Then Brother Zakamlova said, "Brother Lerthansung, the English people put everything in the refrigerator. They keep it cold. We need it warm, so tell him, 'Hot curry, hot curry.'" He meant stove hot.

I told T. Samuel, "Please give us hot curry, hot curry!" Then Brother Samuel brought the curry with chilies. Then he gave some to Brother Zakamlova. Brother Zakamlova was very angry.

"Brother Samuel, I never eat chilies! I come from Mizoram. We never take chilies! Why did you make me these hot chilies?"

Then E. L. Scism said, "You told him, 'We need hot curry.'"

"Oh, I mean. . .hot curry means warm curry. Sometimes we've had cold curry. Very cold. I don't like it. I like it warm. Very warm. So by hot curry I meant warm curry."

The general conference at Adur was attended by some foreign ministers—the Reverend J.Y. Burns and A. W. Post and the Reverend George Shalm from the Apostolic Church of Pentecost of Canada, who later affiliated wih the UPC.

During that conference, we had some interviews with the Reverend W. T. Stairs, the foreign missions director. He occupied one room in the mission bungalow. "I want to hear reports from our district presbyters," he requested.

When I had a chance, I entered his room. Brother Stairs was sitting. "Brother Lerthansung, please come in. Please sit here." When I sat down he continued, "I

Lera

want to hear the report from the Manipur UPC, so please tell me how it began." I started to report as far as I could with my English.

After about fifteen minutes, Brother W. T. Stairs spoke to me, "Brother Lerthansung, can you hear me?"

"Yes, yes, I can hear, sir, but I cannot understand what you say. What to do?"

"I want to hear concerning the Manipur UPC's condition, but I cannot understand what you say. *Please* call your superintendent, Brother E. L. Scism."

"Yes." I went to Brother Scism. "Brother Scism, please help me. Brother W. T. Stairs wants to know about my report, but he cannot understand my English." Then E. L. Scism laughed and he helped me. I spoke in my English, then Brother E. L. Scism translated into the real English. Then Brother Stairs could understand. This was very wonderful.

I needed to make an application for ordination, so I wrote out an application. Brother E. L. Scism said, "After you finish, Brother Zakamlova will give his signature on the bottom."

After I finished, I asked Brother Zakamlova, "Brother Zakamlova, now I am going to take ordination. I already filled out this application. Please help me, please help me." However Brother Zakamlova did not want to sign and asked for a copy.

[Brother Lerthansung had been made district presbyter because he was the most capable person in the district, even though he was not yet ordained by the organization. He had been a district presbyter for four years by this time and was finally asked to apply for his ordination certificate.]

When I told Brother E. L. Scism he said, "I will sign it." He signed for me and gave it to the executive board and it was passed. At that conference, then, Brother Allison Joseph of Nagpur and I were ordained by Brother W. T. Stairs. After ordination, Brother J. Y. Burns gave us some exhortation.

That exhoration has been very, very successful in my life. He said to me, "Brother Lerthansung, now you are ordained to preach the gospel. Some preachers do not have experience, but they want to teach other people. This is very bad, so try to get experience first. Then you can teach other people. Then you will succeed. Wherever you go, many people will ask about some Bible verses. Don't just say your opinion. Try to explain according to the Bible. This is the important thing for you."

From that time, that message I will never forget till my life ends. Wherever I go, I never teach the people if I have no relevant experience. But in that which I have experience, I can teach plainly. God also has helped me so much.

Brothers Masih Das from Bareilly, B. Salins from Mangalore, L. B. Taylor from Madras, A. Joseph from Nagpur, Zakamlova from Mizoram, and T. M. Mathai from Kerala and I from Manipur—we were the first executive board. All those pastors have passed away now, and some left our UPC. Of all of them, I alone am living and active in the UPC today, so I think that I have had special consideration from God. This conference in Adur in March 1958 was the first general conference to have representatives from Northeast India. (The first general conference for mainland India was in 1950.)

After having a good conference at Adur, we went

Lera

back home. Brother Harry Scism led us to the Kottarakara Rail Station and we booked a third-class ticket to Madras. When the train arrived, it was impossible to enter from the door, but Brother Harry Scism helped us enter through the window and gave us our bedding through the window. Lastly, he gave some money for our children and said goodbye.

We reached Madras safely, but we didn't know the city, so we did not want to roam around too much. That evening we left Madras for Calcutta, again with a third-class ticket.

Ministers visiting Adur, Kerala, for the 1958 general conference of India. Front row, left to right: Lerthansung, J. Y. Burns, B. Sallins, Jeyaraj, Zakamlova and Grace Uddas and her mother. Back row, left to right: W. T. Stairs, A. W. Post, Masih Das, George Shalm, Harry Scism, Audrene Scism, Marjorie Scism, Ferne Scism and Ellis Scism.

29 (1964-1986)

Mainland India II

Some time later I went again to Kerala for a conference. In 1964 I came with Brothers Zakamlova and T. R. Challian. When we came down from Calcutta, we could not change our clothes. We were so dirty! We did not know how to get food on the railway either.

When we reached Madras, Brother Zakamlova said, "Now we must put our luggage in the cloakroom. We must try to get a hotel." In front of Egmore Station was the Imperial Hotel. It was very beautiful.

When we entered the reception area, the receptionist looked at me and asked, "Where do you come from?"

"We come from Assam."

"Are you a brother to this man?"

"That is Brother Challian."

"He's so dirty! Such dirty people we do not want to accept in this hotel. See, our hotel is very, very clean."

Due to Brother Challian being so dirty, we could not get into the hotel. Then Brother Zakamlova was very angry. "Brother Challian, due to your dirtiness we can-

Lera

not get food."

Brother Challian responded, "Oh, if this Imperial Hotel does not accept me, my wife will accept me." We went to another hotel and were able to eat.

When we came back from Adur, Brother Challian and Brother Zakamlova had a great disagreement. There were too many passengers on the train; overbooking is common in India. When we would get up from our seat, some other passenger would want to sit there suddenly.

Brother Zakamlova stayed in the upper berth. One day, between Calcutta and Gauhati, Brother Zakamlova went to the bathroom. While he was gone, a young man came and lay down in his place. I told that young man, "Brother, this is Brother Zakamlova's seat. When he comes back, you will have to give it up."

When Brother Zakamlova came back, he saw the young man. At first he requested politely, "This is my seat from Calcutta. Please come down. Please move from here."

But that fellow did not want to move. "No, I want to sleep. The *whole* night you already slept. This morning I want to sleep." They began to quarrel and struggle with each other.

I interrupted, "Brother Zakamlova, remember we are pastors. If we fight on the railway, it's not so nice."

"Oh, Brother Lerthansung, what shall I do? If I beat him, it is not so good because we are district pastors, but he doesn't want to move. What to do? I want to leave my pastorate. I want to fight."

Then I faced that fellow. "Brother, look. This old man came from a far country and feels tired. If you don't move away from this seat, what will happen if he dies?" I scolded him as best as I could. Finally he moved from the seat.

We were very troubled. Brother Challian said, "Brother Zakamlova, this is very bad. You scolded me for my dirtiness, but this fighting is not so good. You are a pastor. He's an ordinary young man. How are you going to fight him?" At last we reached Gauhati and then Silchar, where we parted. I went to Imphal and they went to Aizawl, Mizoram.

Also in 1964 Brother Harry Scism while he was in Bhopal had a Bible seminar. He greatly loved me. There was no need for me to go to the seminar, but he told me, "You need to learn to ride a motorbike. We will give you this Jawa motorcycle. It's very good." So I went to Bhopal.

Brother Harry Scism gave me some instructions for the road. I learned that, then he taught me how to drive. First I sat in back, and he drove about two miles. While he drove, he said, "See, this is the handle, that is the gear, this is. . . ." Thus he taught me on the way, slowly, slowly.

When we came back, Brother Harry Scism said, "All right, brother, now you can drive. You must sit in front. I will sit in the back." Then I held the handlebars. By the help of God I could drive slowly, slowly, slowly. I was very happy because I had a good teacher.

After one week we went to the district transport office to take an examination for the license. When we went up to the district transport officer, Brother Harry Scism talked to him. The officer believed him and trusted him. "If you already taught him, then there's no need to test him. If he knows the road rules, I will give him a license," he said. Easily we got driving licenses through Brother Harry Scism. I was very happy.

Lera

At that time there was a brother who had come from South Mizoram, from the very corner near Burma. At that time he prophesied something, so we called him Prophet Darawia.

He did not want to button his shirt. He left it completely open, and his T-shirt was very, very dirty. The students said, "We cannot force him. If we tell him to button up, then he does not want to obey what we say. Brother Lerthansung, please try to control this Brother Darawia, Prophet Darawia. Since you are a senior pastor he will obey you. He will fear you." I was thirty-seven at the time.

At dinner I stood up and addressed the students. "Brothers, listen to me. I want to talk concerning Darawia. He does not want to use buttons. Brother Darawia is a prophet, so everything he does is an illustration. His shirt he does not want to button; this also is an illustration. This means that salvation is open for all people. He wants to show this practically, so he does not want to button his shirt."

Brother Darawia was very happy. "Yes, yes, Brother Lerthansung. He knows the reason why I do not want to button my shirt. He knows the reason very well."

"But salvation will be closed soon. When Jesus comes back, salvation will be closed. For that reason, tomorrow Brother Darawia will start buttoning his shirt."

Brother Darawia was very happy, and the next day he buttoned his shirt. All the people laughed. From that time on Brother Darawia said, "You alone understood my position, so I want to sit with you when we take food."

Brother Darawia liked *dahl* (lentils) very much. Brother Harry Scism distributed beautiful neckties, foreign neckties. Such kind we had never received before, but Brother Darawia sometimes did not want to put on even such a beautiful kind of necktie. Sometimes he did not want to fix his hair properly or wash his hands.

Pastor Rodinga, who came from North Mizoram, liked Brother Darawia's necktie very much and offered, "If you do not want to put on your necktie properly, *please* give it to me. I will give you my share of dahl for one week."

Brother Darawia was very happy. "All right, all right. I will give you my necktie. Then you must give me your share of dahl. Yes, yes." So he gave his necktie to Brother Rodinga, and for one week Brother Rodinga gave his share of dahl to Brother Darawia. Brother Darawia was very happy. We had come from the hill country and had never experienced or seen so many kinds of dahl. For that reason Brother Darawia liked very much dahl.

This was our condition in Bhopal when we were learning the Bible and motorcycle.

[Within a year, that Bible seminar became Calvary Bible Institute, which moved to Landour, Uttar Pradesh, near the town of Mussoorie, in 1970 and to Shillong in 1973, where it remains. Brother Lerthansung, due to his heavy district duties, was unable to attend the Bible college for several years. Another factor in the decision to delay his enrollment was the greater need to train other students to join senior pastors such as he in the field. However, he continued to visit occasionally our home at 89 Malaviya Nagar, Bhopal, Madhya Pradesh, for years, making possible the following memories of those days in late 1966.]

One day we visited Sanchi with our superintendent, Brother Harry Scism. All the students wondered when they saw the temple of Buddha there. Sanchi is about thirty miles out of Bhopal, and there stands a Buddhist stupa dating back to 50 BC, perhaps the earliest significant standing monument of Buddhism. We were happy to see this.

When we came back from Sanchi, some of our students went to the bazaar. They wanted to purchase something, but they could not speak in Hindi, so sometimes we had great trouble with the Bhopal people. But by the help of God, we had no fighting at all.

One time we had open-air meetings in Bhopal for the Malaviya Nagar church. The superintendent requested me to preach. I preached about the second coming of Jesus Christ. That night I mentioned Israel. "Brothers and sisters, Jesus is coming soon. According to the Bible, Jesus said to learn from the fig tree. The fig tree symbolizes Israel's people. Now the Israeli people have come back to their own country."

Later, a CID man came to me. "Brother, you need not talk about the Israeli people. If you want to speak about the Israeli people, you cannot preach the gospel. In the government, we never exalt or admire the Israeli people." (As a matter of international politics, for many years India did not recognize Israel as a nation.)

I stopped using that point and took up another point.

While in Bhopal we went to the Intkheri camp meeting.

[Intkheri was a village about a day's journey from Bhopal, where Brother T. Samuel had started a church. The Bhopal church had been lacking the spiritual power that their pastor, Brother Harry Scism, wanted to see, so he organized a camp meeting in this village. The whole congregation went out there. Many people spoke in tongues unknown to them but which other people present did know. Brother Vinod Timothy spoke in Malayalam, a language of South India. Sister John, who knew no English, spoke fluently in it. Of special interest to Lerthansung was another case.]

At that time Sister Renu received the Holy Spirit and spoke in other tongues. Brother Harry Scism called out, "Let Brother Damhuala and Brother Saikawlal come." Brother Muana was also there. Then we heard her speaking. She spoke very well in Mizo. She said, "Forgive us. We have already sinned. Please forgive us." She spoke in Mizo very, very clearly.

Later we said, "Please speak to us," but she did not know Mizo. Sister Renu spoke in Mizo, just like the man in East Manipur who prayed in Mizo very, very clearly. These two times I have had such an experience.

Because Brother Harry Scism and his family moved in 1970, we had no opportunity to go back to Bhopal. We first had Bible school in Landour in 1970. I was busy in our Central District, which comprised Meghalaya, Assam, and other areas. I needed to visit every village in my region, so I couldn't go to Bible school. Finally, in 1971 I went to Landour for Bible school.

We had more than sixty students. The district presbyters lived in one room, and the other students lived together in another place.

During Bible school, many wonderful things happened. Once Pastor Sehkholam suffered from stomach pains. He thought he was dying. We didn't know what to do, so we reported to our superintendent. Our superintendent said, "Better take him down to the

Lera

hospital." Six people could hardly carry him, for Brother Sehkholam is a fat man—very heavy by Indian standards. Anyhow, we took him to the car, and then carried him from the car to the hospital.

When he saw the doctors moving here and there, he said, "No, I do not want to stay here. I'm quite all right." When he stood up, he was quite all right, and we did not need to carry him back. By himself he came back.

[He had been sent down there with two other students who had also reported sick but who had at least walked to and from the car. The doctor admitted the other two in the hospital as they were quite ill but told Sehkholam he had stomach gas and to go home.]

When we reported this to the superintendent, our superintendent laughed and laughed. So we don't know the real reason why he got better—either Brother Sehkholam feared the hospital or God touched him—we don't know. Even now we still sometimes joke about it.

[When Brother Harry Scism goes back to that area or meets with the brethren elsewhere, sometimes during a gathering he will coolly, yet mischievously, give a sidelong glance at Sehkholam. Everyone knows what's coming, but Brother Scism's timing is perfect. At precisely the right moment, he will ask Brother Sehkholam if he is still well. This recurring drama has made both men legends in their own time.]

The people who came from Mizoram and Manipur had never visited beyond their area before, so when they gathered together, all the pastors began to talk to each other. "This Landour we did not know before. It is very, very far. I do not know if we can reach our villages again."

When we hill people saw the many, many monkeys

Mainland India II

in Landour, some of the students made a petition. "Sometimes we do not have meat. Anyhow, we hill people like monkeys very much. If our superintendent will permit us, we want to kill them and make curry."

Brother Damhuala asked Brother Harry Scism, "Our students want to kill a monkey. They like it very much. What should we do? If you permit us, we want to kill one."

Brother Harry Scism said, "I have no objection, but the people here love and worship these monkeys. If they know you killed a monkey, then there may be some trouble among the local people. If you want to kill one, then you must kill secretly." Unfortunately, since we had no guns, we could not kill monkeys, and we could not use them to prepare our curry.

All our students liked very much to roam, but we feared our superintendent. Especially our Mizo people cannot keep still. We cannot sit still more than one hour. We want to roam here and there. When we finished our class, sometimes our dean said, "You need not go to the bazaar," but secretly all the students after class went down to the town for shopping. Those who had no money also wanted to go. Sometimes we met our superintendent and we were very embarrassed.

In 1971, when I was at Landour, Uttar Pradesh, for Bible school, I received a letter from my family. "Without school uniforms, the children are not permitted even to enter the classroom. Therefore please consider money for that." Unfortuately I had no money left.

At that time, under Brother Harry Scism, we had fasting and prayer every Saturday. I had a special subject for fasting and prayer—school uniforms. After two weeks Sister Audrene Scism, Mrs. Reverend Harry E.

Lera

Scism, asked me. "Brother Lerthansung, how many daughters do you have?"

"Four daughters."

"We received some clothing and blouses for my daughter, Loretta. Since she is growing up, some blouses are too small, so I want to give you some blouses. They are all white." My children needed white blouses for their school uniforms, so my fasting and prayer to God were answered through Brother Harry Scism's wife.

When we students were returning from Landour, when we reached Dehra Dun, all our luggage we put together in one place. Then we tried to get reserved seats, but we could not control some of our people.

After we got in the rail compartment, we went out and tried to bring them back. Some of them went out another way, so we were in much trouble before we left Dehra Dun. At last, fortunately, we found our students. Then we were able to go back to our homes.

On the way some of our students wanted to fight some plains people. We told them, "Since we are students, and not only students, but since we belong to the United Pentecostal Church ministry, we must not fight other people. If we are fighting, then they will blame us and say the people of the UPC fight other persons. If they say these things, it is not so nice. If our superintendent finds out these things, he will not be happy." It was very difficult to control them while we went back. On the way, sometimes we had singing together, sometimes we had prayer together, and sometimes we almost were fighting together. But at last, by the help of God, we reached our home towns.

In 1972 we went back to the Landour Bible school.

That time also there were more than sixty students. That time also we were very, very busy with Bible study.

One of the brothers who came was a joker. When we had a farewell meeting, he did some joking. He did not know English, but he wanted to say something in English, so our superintendent, Brother Scism, asked him to say something in English. That fellow, when he stood up, said in English, "I will be superintendent, and all of you people will be students. Then I will teach you the Bible as our superintendent teaches us." Then he taught us in English. We almost died laughing. He started in English and then used some strange words. All the people laughed and laughed.

[During one of the two school years that Brother Lerthansung attended Bible college in Landour, Mrs. Daisy "Auntie" Lewis visited our home. When her birthday celebration—we dared not ask how many had preceded it—came, Lerthansung was asked to say a few words. In his inimitable way, he began. The humor crescendoed. The good will in the room was so real that "you could bite into it and chew it like gum," to quote Clemens. Soon almost everyone was chortling over their *chai* (tea) and bellowing over their biscuits at Lerthansung's funny verbal and facial expressions. In addition to his intentionally funny message and the naturally funny, hyperactive dimple he possesses, his accidentally funny grammar added extra humor, since he had been using masculine pronouns in reference to Auntie Lewis. The whole combination was too much, and we required some time afterward to regain our composure.]

That year Brother Harry Scism had a particular burden for our area of the country. "According to your

Lera

reports, you have great numbers, but according to your report those who receive the Holy Spirit are very, very few. It is not so good. This year we are going to have a big crusade again for Northeast India." We had formed evangelistic groups. In my group was Brother Lalhmudik. These crusade teams were very, very successful.

Brother Lalhmudik and I went to northeast Mizoram. We had never visited in that area, the very corner, near the boundary of Burma. In a big village, called Phuoibuong, there was a high school. When we said some English words, many people loved it very much.

Brother Lalhmudik told me, "Some things I will say in English, but if they ask what my qualifications are, you need not tell them." Brother Lalhmudik attended school only to class four, but he put on his necktie nicely and dressed nicely and he could nicely sing. Sometimes he spoke many words in English, so many people respected him.

"Oh, he's a good man; he's a pastor."

"Yeah, I think he can speak very well in English."

Many people asked me, "What are his qualifications?"

"I do not know exactly, but he's an educated person," I told them.

Then we had open-air meetings. The pastors of other churches were very angry. In that village there were pastors for two organizations—the Presbyterian church and the Independent Church of India. The Independent Church of India had twelve hundred members in their congregation. Their pastor was Pastor Saphois. When we had an open-air meeting, only five people attended their church; all the others came to our open-air meeting. Their pastor was very angry and scolded them. "Pastor

Lalhmudik and Pastor Lerthansung visited us. They had an open-air meeting. There were no seats, but many people went to sit in that place. You have left our church. I am so angry. If you want to be rebaptized, we have lots of water in the river. I will baptize you."

I told Brother Lalhmudik, "Last night only five people attended the Independent Church of India, so their pastor is very angry. We need to go to his home." In the early morning, we woke up and went. The pastor had come outside and was passing water. There is no latrine there; the people simply pass water in the street.

When he saw me a little distance away, he entered in his house, then out the back he ran away. When we entered we asked the children, "Where is your father?"

"Oh, he went out the back. He might be in the garden." We waited and waited, but he did not come back. When I looked in his garden he was not there; he had run away. He did not want to speak to us, he was so angry.

On Sunday, we appealed to the people. "Just hearing cannot save you. We need to obey the truth. For those who want to obey the truth, tomorrow we are going to have a baptismal service." Then God blessed us. Forty-seven people took water baptism. We had a great discussion with the other church leaders, but God helped us and they could not defeat us.

Those taking water baptism, including children, were more than sixty. We started a church building. In the hills it is not difficult to make a building. There is plenty of sun grass, plenty of bamboo, plenty of wood. Within five days we had finished the church. A church like that costs only about five hundred rupees because freely we can get the material. The building was thirty by twenty-four feet.

Lera

Everything we got from the jungle freely.

On the finishing day, we wanted to make a feast. During the building of the church, we purchased some chickens. There was no sugar in that area, but there was sugar cane. Milk was not available, so we made "red tea"—*lalchai*. We like it very much. A cup of red tea and sugar cane—it's very, very tasty. It is locally made, and the taste is much different from the rest of India. Some people cannot tolerate it. It's a little strong compared to the tea made by the Mizo. Generally the locally made tea is a little stronger than the machine made. Still, some people like it very much.

In 1973 we could not continue the Bible college in Landour because the Scisms needed to move to Manila. So we moved the school to Shillong. Those who did not finish college in Landour came to Shillong to finish.

In 1973 I was both a student and a teacher. I graduated from our Bible school in 1973 and was immediately appointed as a teacher. I was vice principal for four years. In 1986 Brother Satinvela said, "You and I need to be free from the Bible school. Since we have a full-time Bible principal, Brother Vankunga, our general secretary, can be vice principal, because he does not need to move out from our station in Shillong. You and I need to go out freely."

"Yes, yes. That is good." So from 1986 Brother Vankhunga has been the vice principal in Shillong.

[The pieces begin to fit in place. A missions director with experience in pastoral, missionary, and administrative work nears retirement and gains increasing freedom of movement. When an opening arises in the nation of India, he, having Bible school and evangelistic experience there, is equipped to lead Bible college graduates in doing the work of an evangelist to fulfill the Great Commission throughout the Indian subcontinent. How marvelous is God's plan!]

In October 1985 Brother Kawlthuama, Brother L. C. Sailo, and I went to Delhi. There we met Brother Stanley Scism. From Delhi we went down to Bhopal, and from Bhopal to Intkheri. We had good meetings in Inkheri.

[We wanted a new revival in North India to begin, for the Holy Spirit to come on us just as it had come on them in the beginning in 1966. (See Acts 11:15.) We even had our own Apostle Peter, since Lerthansung was present at both events. Brother Kawlthuama preached the first night. The young people had the Saturday morning service. The power fell on Saturday night when Brother Lerthansung preached. Back in 1966, villagers had seen fire atop our church building and had come in afraid. This time, Vijay Singh, while he was receiving the Holy Spirit, saw a vision of fire surrounding the building. People were healed, delivered and released. It was beautiful. Brother L. C. Sailo preached Sunday morning, and I spoke Sunday night, after which we had communion and footwashing, the sacrament being administered by the pastor of the local church.

In accordance with the Sunday night message on unity, we took the Lord's Supper while seated in the shape of a human body. At the head was the table bearing the communion elements. It was unique, and a lovely final touch to a great camp.]

This was a new experience for me. We have the Lord's Supper and footwashing, but we never do it like we did this time. Brother Stanley washed my feet, and

Lera

I washed his feet. Brother Sailo washed his friend's feet. This was very wonderful for me. Then we sat around for the Lord's Supper also, and some people received the Holy Spirit.

But there was no good bathroom. Sometimes we went to the jungle or to the river. Brother Stanley took baths outdoors. He sacrificed, so I like him very much.

[However, for the Westerner they did put up a temporary toilet facility, two long flat stones about eight inches apart over a hole in the ground, the whole thing surrounded by brush banked up. I kept my underwear on while bathing, which in India is customary, besides being economical, since the clothes and the person are washed simultaneously. I also wore a *lungi* (waist cloth) while bathing. It was no great sacrifice. The river was high, and bathing in rapids is fun, yet relaxing—like having a huge personal whirlpool tub, only without the expense, maintenance, and trouble. Of course, it isn't possible to heat up a river, but in India that's usually no problem.]

We came back to Bhopal (where we said goodbye to the people from Delhi—Robin, George and Anil Kumar) as well as to Brothers Kawlthuama and L. C. Sailo, who went back to Northeast India. From Bhopal we went to Jabalpur. In Jabalpur, we had good meetings. Twelve people received the Holy Spirit there. All the people loved Brother Stanley very much. They did not see him as a foreigner; they saw him as their real friend. They love him and Brother Stanley loves them.

We came back to Bhopal again, where we also had good meetings. Some people from other denominations came and heard our message.

Mainland India II

From Bhopal we went to Indore, where we met Brother Solomon, the former superintendent in mainland India. We helped, and we encouraged him as far as we could to stand firmly for the truth. He told me, "Yes, although I did not hold my superintendency, I will stand firmly for this truth."

After Indore, we went to Nasik. Brother Stanley wanted to see the school where he studied in his childhood. He showed me a tree, saying, "This tree I climbed up." That day he climbed it again.

From Nasik we went to Bombay, and met Pastor Maben. That night I said, "When I was at the Manila conference, thousands and thousands of UPC pastors gathered together. I think that I was the smallest among them. But here, our Pastor Maben is shorter than me by about half an inch. Praise the Lord! Praise the Lord!" I was very happy.

We had good services in Bombay also. Several people received the Holy Spirit. Sometimes we used a lady named Miriam as translator. She did very well, but best of all, she received the Holy Spirit in those meetings.

Then we took a bus to Koppa. We spent more than twenty-eight hours going, going, going. On the way we had no time to take food, no time to drink anything. For me it was not so difficult. But Brother Stanley, he suffered greatly, but by the help of God, he suffered with happiness.

[Maybe it's only retrospect, but I don't remember it being so bad. Sure, it was easier for him than for me in the bus, since he, being smaller, wasn't so cramped for space. On the other hand, I had better company than he did, so that evens the score.]

Lera

When we reached Koppa we had good services and also Bible classes. All the people love Brother Stanley, and he also loves them. They told me, "We receive any visitors, and they present us with good messages, but we have no close relationship with them. We respect them, but we can't have a close relationship. But Brother Stanley—he is like us. We cannot see him as a foreigner. We think he is like us."

After we left Koppa we went to Kodaikanal. We visited a school there, where Brother Stanley met some teachers, but we had no meeting there. From Kodaikanal we came to Madras. In Madras we had a good meeting Sunday. Then we went sightseeing at Mahabalipuram. All the people loved him so much. The atmosphere was also good. My spirit was very happy.

I wanted to visit with him in other places, but since we had programs in Nagaland, I had to leave Brother Stanley. While we visited together, since his English is very good and my English is hopeless, sometimes I learned from him. If we could work together more days, my English would progress so much, I thought. He is a good teacher for me, but since I had other plans, I could not stay any longer. I left him in Madras.

* * * * * * * * *

[I went on to Andhra Pradesh, to a church which hadn't been visited and encouraged from the outside since 1962. It is no wonder that the Madras church is in such good shape, considering how much attention and care and money has been poured into it over the years. After visiting Delhi again to get government permits, I returned south through Bhopal and Raipur, where I spent my

Christmas holiday with the Silas family and enjoyed the good Christian spirit of the John family. I was back in Madras for the watchnight service, then went to Sri Lanka for a month. There I taught a Bible class and in churches outside Colombo, the capital city, on weekends. In February I went to Nepal with Brother Nathan Paul and, after a detour to the general conference, went to Sikkim with him. In both places I was the first Western visitor to our new churches there. By March I had finished all this plus an evangelistic program in Calcutta, and was heading, via Jabalpur and Bhopal, back to Delhi. In Delhi, I met my parents, where we made inquiries about residential visas then went to Landour, near Mussoorie, for the same purpose I had gone to Kodai—to see if it was possible to obtain visas for American schoolteachers. After returning to Delhi, we negotiated for the purchase of the new Bible college, advanced training center and local church property. This place, the Lord willing, will become a magnificent tool to unite efforts in India toward a national evangelistic thrust. After my parents left Delhi, I went to Calcutta, where I met Brother Lerthansung again.

Brother Lerthansung and I flew to the Andaman Islands, an Indian territory in the middle of the Bay of Bengal, which in British days was a penal colony. Soon after our arrival, we were informed by the CID officer that I was not to engage in religious activity, and our pastor, Fouj Singh, was warned not to take me to any churches. Accordingly, we canceled services to be held at the Lutheran church where we had hoped to talk about the one true God. During the resulting free time, I sat down with Brother Lerthansung and interviewed him on

Lera

cassette, thus providing most of the material for this book. We did a couple of days' touring to convince the authorities that we were tourists, then on Sunday spoke in a house meeting in town, where several denominational people heard the truth. We returned to Calcutta and said goodbye at the Howrah rail station.]

Lerthansung speaking in Delhi, Robin translating (1985).

30 (1986)
Missions Work

After parting with Brother Stanley Scism in Calcutta, I went to Arunachal Pradesh on April 24, 1986, to preach the full gospel. Along with Sister Zoramthari, Bible woman from West Siang District, we went to East Siang District. God moved the people's hearts in East Siang District so that eight people took water baptism in the name of Jesus.

Meanwhile, I had to leave Arunachal on May 5 since my inner line permit was no longer valid. During the night, I left Arunachal Pradesh. C. Chawngbula took me along in his jeep, and we proceeded through Assam State.

About 8:00 PM, we came through a thick forest where there were many wild animals such as elephants, tigers and bears. While we were driving in the thick forest, we saw one elephant standing at the roadside. The moment the elephant heard the sound of our jeep, he came towards the sound making a lot of noise. I told the driver to drive at a fast speed, and fortunately the elephant could not catch us.

Lera

After driving ten minutes, we saw another elephant standing just near the roadside. After hearing the sound of the jeep, he came toward the light and blew with loud noises, but I told my friends not to be scared for the Lord is always with those who preach His true full gospel. By God's help we were able to pass safely once again.

Brother C. Chawngbula told me that the elephants in this area are very wild and that an elephant recently caught hold of a jeep and broke it into pieces. Although some people may lose their lives in this area because of the elephants, yet God is always with me and safely we entered Assam State. Proverbs 18:10 says, "The name of the LORD is a strong tower: the righteous runneth into it, and is safe." Praise the Lord, he has fulfilled this verse in a practical way in my life. I am reminded of how God was with Daniel and saved him from the lions' den.

From July to September 1986 I taught in Bible school and took the subjects of Evangelism and Teaching Techniques. During this Bible school period, I wrote a book in Mizo called *The Deity of Jesus Christ*. Brother Sangzuala Sailo helped me in printing and two thousand copies were published. Through this book, many people came to know about the one true God and within a period of just four months more than fifty people accepted the Oneness of God and took water baptism in Jesus' name. God has really blessed the book, and right now I'm preparing to enlarge it for a reprint. If possible, I'm trying to reprint it in Mizo and Hmar. As far as other languages are concerned, I'm planning to print it again as soon as money is available for printing.

At the request of the executive board of Northeast India I have also written several books over the years on

Sunday school subjects: I and II Corinthians, Galatians, Ephesians, Philippians, Colossians, the Tabernacle, children's Sunday school subjects (in Hmar), Christian women, and my autobiography.

Soon after the Bible school term was over, I went up to Mizoram to attend our missions conference and crusade. First we had a missions conference at Champhai, near the Burma border, and next we had one at Lunglei, South Mizoram. The missions funds we raised during our conferences in Champhai and Lunglei came to twelve thousand rupees. I am so glad that our members have a greater burden for lost souls than before. It is indeed a pleasure to see the people having a great missionary vision. During our conference and crusade, forty people took water baptism in Jesus' name and many people received the gift of the Holy Ghost.

On November 6-9, I went to Gangtok, Sikkim, to attend the UPC conference there. We call this area a missions field, and the people are Nepali. Brother Stanley Scism had once visited this very place and preached in a service. It was the first time for the people to see a white minister from the UPC, and they were really happy to see him and honored him very much. According to some viewers, they found him so handsome a young man that they expect him to be the most handsome among the Americans.

From Darjeeling and Kalimpong, twenty delegates came, and the leaders of the Elsadai Church and the Independent Pentecost, Brothers D. K. Gurung and Ranzing Bal, also attended our meeting. They have heard the full gospel now. They told me that though they've been leaders of their churches, yet they have never before heard the necessity of taking water baptism in Jesus' name for the remission of sin. So, along with six others, these two church leaders took water baptism in Jesus' name. These two further told me, "Pastor, at this Sikkim conference God has sent you specially for us. Through you we came to know the truth, and we would like to bring all our church members to this truth." It is really a great thing that a UPC pastor can baptize a trinitarian pastor. After our conference was over, God safely took me back to Shillong again.

An old lady was healed after hearing about my ministry, as the following letter relates.

December 1, 1986

My dear father in Christ, Lerthansung:
Greetings in the name of Jesus:

While I was in North Vanlaiphai Village, an old lady came to me to pray for her sickness. She had a big ball like a boil under her jaw and was running a high temperature. Before I prayed for her, she inquired about your wonderful ministry, and I began to narrate about your wonderful ministry in detail to her. To my great surprise, suddenly she stopped my speaking and said that she had been completely healed of her sickness while she was yet listening to me about your ministry. She said that it was enough for her and there would be no necessity to pray for her sickness. Being excited and thrilled with joy, I am writing this letter to you.

May God use you more in ministry.
Yours in Christ,

C. Lalnunmawii
Tarpho Village,
S. Mizoram.

Through this letter from Sister Lalnunmawii, Bible woman, God really proved to me that He can do anything and that nothing is impossible for Him. We also find in the Bible that sick people, after seeing Peter and John's happy, willing ministry, were healed. Thus it is important for us ministers to sacrifice our lives more and more to God.

I was asked to speak about Christmas on an All-India Radio broadcast for December 21, 1986. I divided the topic into four feats of Jesus and had five hundred copies printed in both the Mizo and Hmar languages:

1. Bethelehem	Feat of Humility
2. Time of Demonstration (earthly ministry)	Feat of Unification—He is God and man.
3. Calvary	Feat of Redemption by his death, burial and resurrection. Our identification with His work is by repentance, baptism in Jesus' name, and baptism in the Holy Spirit.
4. Mt. Olivet	Feat of the Great Commission to preach the full gospel to every creature in the world.

Lera

On December 5-8, 1986, Brother Harry Scism's family, with the exception of his daughter, Loretta, came up to Manipur, and the executive board of Northeast India went up from Shillong to Manipur. I took my wife along with me for she had not seen them for a long time. We were all very happy to see Brother Harry Scism and his family. Their love for the people of Northeast India is so very great.

I praise the Lord that Brother Harry Scism and his family went to Chakpikarong! On the morning of December 7 they, along with the executive board, went to Chakpikarong, East Manipur District, to inspect the school. I was asked to preach at the Churachandpur headquarters church during their absence and so I took this opportunity. That Sunday morning thousands of people came to church in hopes of hearing a message from Brother Harry Scism. It was a privilege for them to see a white man, for they had not seen one for a long time.

Although there were no white men to be seen, yet all the people who came to see and hear the message of Brother Harry Scism attended the meeting till the end. I preached to them about the full gospel and the deity of Jesus Christ. After the service, many people told me that, although they came to hear and see the Americans, it was an opportunity for them to know about the Oneness of God and the full gospel, which they had never heard before. So they praised the Lord because Brother Harry Scism and his family had gone to Chakpikarong.

On Sunday night, many people were waiting for Brother Harry Scism and his family when they came back from Chakpikarong. Then they were able to listen to his message, and many people shook his hand and saw him

Missions Work in 1986

face to face. They had pictures snapped with Brother Harry Scism and his family. Many leaders of other churches asked us, "How can you get permission for your missionaries?" We answered, "By prayer to God."

I have great hope that there will be fruit from this missionary trip to Manipur, both physically and spiritually.

Brother Lalthar, IAS officer from Dimapur, Nagaland, gave a plot of land to the Dimapur UPC to construct a church building. He is the son of one of our elders, Ngama Reiek. On November 10, the church members started construction with nine thousand rupees only, but God was so kind and knowing of our needs. He worked in everyone's heart. Everyone left aside his own personal work and instead gave all his time in building the church. On December 21, 1986, we dedicated the church building. I asked the following four questions, and to each one the congregation responded with an amen.

1. "May I dedicate this church on this day, December 21, 1986, to the glory of God, to be used for the preaching of the one true God, baptism in Jesus' name, the baptism of the Holy Spirit, and the full gospel for salvation of mankind?"

2. "May I dedicate this church to the glory of God, to be used for worship by true worshipers who have received the gift of the Holy Spirit?"

3. "May I dedicate this church to the glory of God, to be used for reconciliation of the wretched sinner with God divine?"

4. "May I dedicate this church to the hand of God for full protection from the wicked and from calamities and accidents?"

On the night of December 26, 1986, some ladies came

Lera

to our evening service at the UPC headquarters in Shillong. They stayed with us that night. Our Pastor Nathan Paul told them about the one true God and baptism in Jesus' name. Three ladies accepted baptism in Jesus' name, so we had a baptismal service on the morning of December 27, and they went back to their village with great joy. These Khasi sisters came from Smith Area, which is about nine miles from Shillong. I thank the Lord that our gospel truth is now spreading among the Khasi people.

[As this book wraps up, I look forward to further opportunities to work with Brother Lerthansung on the Indian subcontinent. When working together, we seem to bring out the good in each other. My association with him as an adult and co-worker and back in my teens and childhood—and even before that, in that he first came to Kerala about a month before I was born—leaves me admiring and respecting him as a leader in the Lord and a true soldier. I have asked him to talk about the family that has stood behind him and remained faithful to the Lord despite all the strains caused by having a father who is frequently on the road—a condition with which I can well sympathize.]

Saikawt, near Churachandpur—the first church in that area. Lerthansung was visiting here when God told him to go back to his wife, who was about to have a miscarriage.

31

My Family Through the Years

I have six children—four daughters and two sons. When we moved to Churachandpur, my wife had a miscarriage and a daughter was born dead. Yet a miracle happened that night.

That night Saikant Village requested me to visit their village to preach. I went by bicycle. When I reached Saikant, before I entered in the chapel, I heard in my heart, "Go back, go back, go back."

I wondered, Here I'm going to preach the gospel, but all I can think of is to go back. I couldn't tolerate it. I told the pastor, "Pastor, I came to Saikant Village to preach, but—I don't know the real reason—when I reached Saikant Village, my heart said, 'Go back, go back, go back, go back.' If I preach here tonight, I will not succeed. If you have no objection, I will go back to my home town, Churachandpur."

The pastor replied "If you feel like that, you may go back to Churachandpur."

Lera

When I reached my home, about 8:30 PM, my wife was in much pain. "Why did you come back so soon?" she asked.

"Just before I reached the chapel, my heart was full of 'Go back, go back, go back.' I could not tolerate it, so I told Brother T. R. Challian I wanted to go back to my home. I came back so soon because I did not preach in the chapel."

"Yes, that is good. That means God called you back. Just after you left the home, I had stomach pains. It is not time to deliver yet, for it's only been about six months. But I had so much stomach pain. I could not call for other people either." My wife was in so much pain, and I did not know what to do. At that moment, my wife miscarried. I checked the baby; it was a girl.

I wrapped the baby in a small cloth. When I cleaned it, according to our custom, I did not want to invite other people. I said to myself, "I will make a grave near our house. Then I can keep our baby." We hill people, when our wives miscarry, never go to the cemetery. We make a small grave near our house, so in the night I made the small grave myself.

Just before I put the baby in, a big dog came and took my daughter. Since I wanted to get the baby back, I ran as far as I could for about two hundred yards. At last I recovered my daughter's body.

One of my friends named Buonga woke up and came out. "What is the reason, Pastor, that you make such a great sound?"

"Unfortunately my wife miscarried tonight. I prepared a grave, but just before I put the baby in, the dog took it away. Then I tried to take it back from the dog.

My Family Through the Years

For that reason I made some sounds."

Brother Buonga said, "According to our neighborhood by-laws, you must tell two or three neighbors. They will prepare a grave, and then they'll bury the body. We never do it ourselves."

"I did not know. Our own custom is that when we have trouble, we do not want to make trouble for other people. I was thinking that way."

Brother Buonga helped me, then we finished our work.

By the help of God my wife did not have that kind of trouble again. Since I have practice and training, when my wife delivered, we never called a nurse and never went to the hospital. Since I was convenient, I helped my wife. I did not want to call other people, because I had some experience.

This was my family's condition when I was in Churachandpur.

As far as I can, I want to follow the Bible. When we were to move to Churachandpur, our church people in Senvon had a committee meeting. "We are a very new organization in Senvon village. We have no good place for the church building. What shall we do?" they asked.

My house's location was very central and very convenient. I said, "Yes, God gave me the Holy Spirit. I want to give back something to the Lord. My house and my plot I will give to the church." Then I handed over my house to the church. We were very happy.

When I moved again from Churachandpur to Cachar, I had a small house near our church. Just before we transferred, our church committee made a resolution. "Brother Lerthansung, since you are moving to Cachar

Lera

and since your house is very, very close to our church, if you surrender it to the church, we shall be happy." When I had built the church, for my house Brother E. L. Scism had helped me with about four hundred rupees.

I had a small house. I thought, "If the church committee made a resolution, then I have no objection. I will hand over my house to the United Pentecostal Church." So I handed over my second home.

When we reached Hmarkolien, we rented a house. Then we purchased a house for the United Pentecostal Church, and I occupied mission quarters. When we moved from Cachar to Shillong, we rented a house again.

Sometimes my sons and daughters have to give an address to the government. "Where is your address, your home address?" they are asked.

"We have no home address. We are like birds flying. Right now we inhabit Shillong, Meghalaya."

I say, "You should tell them your home address is in Shillong, Meghalaya." Thus when my children or I need to write a home address, we use Shillong, which is neither our tribal nor even our linguistic area.

Now I want to introduce my family. I was born in 1927. My parents couldn't read or write, but they knew the month and year of my birth. "In the first month you were born, but we do not know the exact date. We never recorded it."

When I applied for an international passport, it was necessary to write down my birthday. That application was in 1972 in Delhi. What shall I do? I thought. If I write down the wrong date that will be a lie, and how can a pastor lie?

My Family Through the Years

Brother Harry Scism advised, "Brother Lerthansung, this is not so bad. I will give you your birthday. Since you were born in the month of January, it will be easy to remember. The Indian government has a great holiday day January 26. This is Republic Day. You should use January 26 for your birthday."

When we filled out our passport applications, I put my birthday—"26 January 1927." So, from that time, I use it as my birthday. Sometimes I say, "Brother Harry Scism is like a second god because he arranged my birthday. I am very happy because it is very convenient for me. If we say January 6 or 7, sometimes I will forget. But since we have a liberation holiday on January 26 I can always remember, "Oh, this is my birthday!"

My wife was born in 1930, but at that time her father was not able to read or write, so he did not know the exact date. So I gave a birthday to my wife. "Brother Harry gave me my birthday, so your birthday will be January 14."

We married in 1948. By the help of God on January 6, 1949, we had a son. We called him Dinga. Although I never use our surname, Tryte, my son calls himself Dinga Tryte.

By the help of God, when we came to Shillong, he wanted to become a policeman, so he joined the police department. In 1974, when we had general conference in Shillong, Brother and Sister Harry Scism and Brother and Sister Tenney attended our general conference. Before the conference, I asked the advice of Brother Harry Scism. "We are going to have a marriage for my son. What do you think about having it during our conference? That will be good if you have no objection."

Lera

Brother Harry said, "Yes, yes. No harm. We must plan the general conference to include the marriage service. It is good. Brother T. F. Tenney will be coming. If you have no objection, please request him to perform the marriage. Then you will see what the American custom is."

We were very happy. During the general conference, my eldest son got married and Brother T. F. Tenney performed the marriage. So many people, including non-Pentecostals, wanted to see it. "Ah, an American will perform the marriage," they said. They wanted to see the different style.

Brother Tenney stood together with his wife. They held Bibles. After the marriage service, they gave encouragement. Brother Tenney read out of the Bible for Dinga, and his wife read out of the Bible for Dinga's wife. When we saw this, we liked it very much.

I don't know what the reason is, but until now they have had no child. After ten years I wrote a letter to Brother T. F. Tenney. "My eldest son up till now has no child. *Please* pray for them so they can get a child." Still, until now they haven't received a child.

My second son we call Sanga Tryte. He was born in 1953. When I had my first child, I left my house to go to Bible school. In 1952 I came back to my home.

Unfortunately, Sanga did not succeed in the B.A. final examination.

[The Indian system of education, copying the British, is woefully inadequate on this point. A student may do all the course work well, but his grade depends solely on his performance on the final examination. The tension is incredible around examination time, and this in itself causes many good students to do poorly. On the one hand, the system does counteract poor teaching and favoritism in the local classroom and does prepare students for pressure they'll meet in future job examinations; on the other hand, it makes teachers teach toward the test, thus eliminating other learning activities and life preparation in the classroom. Anyway, "even though it seems absurd, that's the way it is."]

I thought, I have a good friend in the service of India's central government. I need to get a job for my son. I went to the director, Mr. Vankhuma. "My second son did not succeed in the B.A. examination. What to do? I am working in the United Pentecostal Church. I get only a little help. I have six children. If you can arrange something for my second son..."

Brother Vankhuma responded, "We have a vacancy for the survey office of India as a storekeeper. But he needs to go to Hyderabad in mainland India for about six months."

"Oh, no harm, no harm. If you can accept him, then I will send him to Hyderabad for training. This is good." So my second son joined the service of India in 1975 and went to Hyderabad for training.

Three years after he came back, we needed to move to Nagaland. We would have to leave him alone in Shillong, so we thought it would be better for him to get married. If he was alone, it would not be so good.

Fortunately, we found a suitable girl from Churachandpur who was in college. We made an agreement with her parents. According to our custom, I went to Churachandpur and paid the bride price. In Churachandpur, though these people were Mizo, the price was a little high. In Mizoram, the price is about four hundred, but in Churachandpur it was one thousand rupees.

[Decades ago, the bride price had more monetary significance. It has not by any means kept up with inflation, and no longer represents the payment of expenses for rearing the daughter about to become one's wife. Nowadays, the bride price is a symbol of appreciation, saying, "We thank you for bringing up this lovely girl to be our son's companion. Here is a token of our gratitude."]

After our agreement, we considered how we could get one thousand rupees. Some of our relatives helped me. I brought the money to Churachandpur and I gave it; then they married. By the help of God, my second son and his wife have three children.

My third child is a girl, Dari Tryte. She was born in 1955. When she finished high school, she went to college, but unfortunately, she did not succeed in the B.A. second year examinations. At that time, I had a friend working in the air force. I went to his office. "We need a job for my daughter. She already finished typing and stenography. So, if you could arrange for her. . ."

A high officer said, "Yes, yes. Just now we have four vacancies, two positions for typists." She got the vacancy; when she tested out for it, by the help of God she got first place among the applicants. In 1984 she became a stenographer in the air force.

Then, we received another girl, born in 1958. My wife and I talked together. "Nowadays many people want to give foreign names, English names. So it's better to send a letter to Brother Harry Scism." When she was born, I wrote the letter. "Brother Harry Scism, we have another child, a baby girl. Please give us her name. We are waiting. Before you send her name, we are simply sitting here. We do not want to call her anything or make another name."

Brother Harry Scism wrote to me, "I found a beautiful name in the Bible—Ruth. You will call her Ruth." So we called my second daughter Ruth Tryte. By the help of God, she got a job in the Mizo high school, working as a teacher.

My third daughter was born in 1961. My wife was very happy. "Please write again to Brother Harry Scism for her name." According to my wife's pleasure, I wrote another letter. "Brother Harry Scism, we received another girl. Please again give me her name."

He wrote back, "I have a beautiful name. You will call her Mary." Then we called her Mary Tryte. So for two of my daughters we received beautiful names from Harry Scism.

By the help of God I received another girl. The youngest, she was born in May 1964. During that time, whenever I visited people who looked down on me with spite, they said, "That pastor is a *hlimpawl* pastor." *Hlimpawl* means *revival*. When we say, hlimpawl, they look down on us because we have singing, dancing, and praising and say "Hallelujah" and "Praise the Lord." For that reason they scolded me, saying, "Hlimpawl pastor, hlimpawl pastor."

I told my wife, "If we have another girl, I want to name her Hlimpawli. If it's a son, Hlimpawla, because wherever I go, many people say, 'Hlimpawl pastor.' Some people, when they kill a tiger, use that name. If they have some money, they use their own name. If they are a graduate, they use a name concerning education. Wherever I go, many people say, 'Hlimpawl pastor, hlimpawl pastor.'"

When we received our youngest daughter, I called her Hlimpawli Tryte. This is my youngest daughter. By the help of God, she is a fine girl. Up till now (1986), she's studying in school. This year she's in the final year of her B.A. studies. She's interested very much in playing table tennis. Sometimes she goes to Mizoram to play. In Meghalaya she won the state championship for the last three consecutive years.

Sometimes she appeals to me, "If it is possible, I want to go to Bible school. My brothers and sisters are not working in our church."

What am I to do? Until now we have no room for girls in our Bible school. If there is any way possible, I want to send her somewhere, but where shall I send her? When she appeals to me, it greatly presses my heart. My other sons and daughters are working in the government. I do not want to compel them if they have not heard a call from God. But when my daughter talks about Bible school, I think it might be a call from God, but I don't know where to send her since at this time we have no girls' quarters in our Bible school. Anyhow, I will pray for her. If God has called her, God will arrange for her somehow.

32

Spiritual Children and Spiritual Volleyball

I started my pastoral work in 1955, and during a little over thirty years of service I have so far baptized more than five thousand people and established three new districts. Also, eleven mission fields have been opened, and by the grace of our Lord Jesus I have baptized twenty-two pastors in the name of Jesus. This has been accomplished by the power of God's Spirit and God's Word (Zechariah 4:6; Hebrews 4:12).

In closing, here are two illustrations I often use to encourage missions work. First, if we have one child, we are happy. If we have another, we are more happy. If we have three, we are even more happy. If we have ten, we are more and more happy. "Though I have lots of children, I can't be happy"—we can't say that.

Like that, if we catch one lost soul, we're happy. If we catch another lost soul, we're more happy. According to our work so also is our happiness. The pastors who are

Lera

burdened for lost souls, those who catch many lost souls, are so happy. This we have talked and talked about to the pastors.

Some people, if they have twenty or sixty members, try to be satisfied. But if we have more members, we are more happy.

I have told our pastors about the financial side, also. If we have one child, we purchase one coat, but if we have two children, we need to purchase two. Like that, if we have more workers, we need to give more money. In missions, every year we have more workers, so we need to give more and more.

According to our children we are happy. When a man and a woman get married, they are happy, but they need another happiness—the joy of having children. However, many people, after they get married have no children. Then, if they have no children, sometimes they have quarrels between them. "Because of you we have no child," he'll say. The wife also says, "Because of you we have no child." They have quarrels; if they have no children they are not happy. But those who have great fruit have great joy.

This is another illustration of mine. Some places have a district spirit; some places have a sectional spirit; some places have a local spirit. Wherever I go, I tell them, "We the spiritual people must have spiritual volleyball." In 1950, Brother E. L. Scism hit the volleyball to Mizoram. We heard the truth, and we could not keep quiet. From Mizoram, we gave the gospel truth to Manipur in 1953. From Manipur, since we could not keep quiet, we gave it to Cachar District. Then from Cachar we gave it to Tripura and North Cachar and Shillong. This is spiritual volleyball.

But some pastors, when they hear the truth, do not want to give it out to other places. They keep quiet. Suppose we play vollyball. When the other team sends the ball over, if we hold it, it is an error. Like that, those who hear the truth and have the truth, if they do not send it out, they do not defeat the enemy. Spiritual volleyball is very important. So many pastors and church leaders have a factional spirit; they are not good players in spiritual volleyball.

Sometimes I give this as an example. The people laugh and laugh. But I give not only theory. If we make the truth practical and practice it, then they can understand.

Sometimes I take my example a bit further. During the reign of Saul, the Philistines controlled the ark. When King David came, he brought the ark back from Philistia to Israel. Like that, within the UPC we have the new covenant. The gospel, we can say, is our ark. The trinitarian denominations cannot carry it around. But we Oneness believers, we in the United Pentecostal Church, carry it. And we can carry the gospel to any place.

Lera

MY FAMILY

Front row, left to right: Lerthansung, Hlimpawl, Darchawng, Mary. Back row, left to right: Ruth, Dinga, Sanga, Dari.

Lerthansung receives a warm welcome throughout India.